~~101~~ No 262
Reasons Why the Saints Need to
WITNESS!

BRENDA WILLIAMS

ISBN 978-0-9837566-7-5

Published by
Emerge Publishing Group, LLC
Riviera Beach, FL
877.363.7430
www.emergepublishers.com

Brenda Williams 2012
~~101~~ No 262 Reasons Why The Saints Need To Witness!
1. Religious 2. Inspirational

Printed in the United States of America

DEDICATION

This book is dedicated to:

My husband, Robert and Kids.

My Pastor, Carrie Youmans, 90 years old and still wants an outreach ministry. She's like Caleb who at 85 asked Joshua to give him Hebron.

My mother, Elsie Aiken and brother Alvin.

Carol Rosier, a dear friend and prayer partner.

SPECIAL THANKS

I want to thank Gwen Carbaugh, Patricia Gore, Eboni Reed, Marie Barfield and Pastor Rose Williams for going witnessing with me several times.

Pastor Rose has been doing this for years. Witnessing is her passion also. I thank God for brother Reeves. He's in my church and he goes out witnessing all the time.

Thank God for the prayer line that I'm on—*Life Line Prayer*. It is a powerful prayer team that was started by Minister Sheilia Tucker of Detroit, Michigan. It consists of anointed prayer warriors: her husband, Evangelist Tucker; her mother-in-law, Minister Barbara McNeil; a grandmother-in-law, Mother Johnson who is 90 and keeps giving a Word from the Lord; Sister Sheila Ferguson, Prophetess Carol Rosier, Pastor Rose Williams, and Minister Bruce Hendricks.

Marriages have gotten back together since I've been on this prayer line, even the leaders that had problems in their homes. We've had many miracles, healings, jobs, unexpected money, families united, pregnancies and cancer being healed several times

So if anyone has a problem give Life Line a call Monday through Friday, 6am and 12 noon and Sunday at 6am. The call is free. The number is 1-559-726-1000, access code is 662209#. Push pound button. That's the button under the 9 button to get on. After you give your prayer request push the *6 or mute on your phone. You'll still hear the prayers, but we won't hear you if you're talking or have noise in the background. Call back to give a praise report when your prayer is answered.

Call, your life will change!

CONTENTS

INTRODUCTION 1

CHAPTER 1: Did God Sin? 5

CHAPTER 2: Different Religions 31

CHAPTER 3: God Knows My Heart 43

CHAPTER 4: Rejections 63

CHAPTER 5: God Laughs at Me When I Sin 81

CHAPTER 6: The Deceptions of Satan 91

CHAPTER 7: I Have My Spirit 105

CHAPTER 8: You're Witnessing Wrong 123

CHAPTER 9: My Family 155

CHAPTER 10: Comments From Saved People 173

ABOUT THE AUTHOR 181

INTRODUCTION

One day I was at my oldest daughter's house praying, being so grateful to the Lord for His mercy and loving kindness. I asked the Lord, "What can I do for you?" He put it in my spirit to go around the neighborhood and witness, so I did. Some people received my witness and some didn't. I asked the Lord what to ask people, and he told me to ask them "if they ever thought about being saved."

That was the summer of 1998.

This is How I Approach People:

I would walk up to them or behind them and say, "Excuse me, can I ask you something?" They would say, "Yes." I would say, "Have you ever thought about being saved, giving your life to Jesus?"

If they said yes. I would say that's the Lord giving you that thought, because He has a plan and purpose for your life. That when we live our lives ourself we make a mess. God wants to fix the mess in your life, but he won't do it unless you ask Him to help you. God knows all about you. He has the right spouse, job, and house for you, but He wants you to fall in love with Him.

He'll move heaven and earth for you. God will never break your heart. He will never make you cry; He'll never disappoint you. God is not just some spirit in the sky. He wants you to know Him, to have a personal relationship with Him, whereas He talks to you, guides, leads, comforts and shows you things. I tell them we're living in the last days, with all the wars, crimes and natural disasters. I tell them that the Lord is waiting on you. I also tell them there's a void in everybody's heart that only God can fill.

The longer we stay away from God the worst the void gets. People try drugs, alcohol, sex, try more and bigger things but it doesn't fill the emptiness. It just gets worse. Some people kill themselves instead of giving their life to God. God created us and only God can satisfy us.

I tell them I know you're not ready to give up your ways and sins. We all were born with a sinful nature, and sin comes naturally. Talk to the Lord. Tell Him you are not ready to be saved, but ask Him to help you to give up. Let that be your regular prayer. "Lord help me to give up; save me." You can pray this on your knees, while you are at work or school or walking the street. Keep that prayer in your heart. "Lord help me to give up, save me."

Some would thank me and say they would do that. Some gave me some outrageous answers. I would write down what they said just to keep. On October 2, 2009 the Lord told me to write a book about witnessing and the answers I got. At first I would only witness to older people. I was scared to ask police, lawyers or anyone high class or in a suit. I prayed for boldness. Now I'll ask anybody. Just about everyday I witness when I go somewhere.

We are the true witnesses of Jesus Christ. A lot of people will never set foot in a church. We're the church. We need to go out to them. We as saints-people whom God has made holy-need to follow Jesus's example. He didn't stay in the synagogue but walked about spreading the gospel.

I'm praying for a passion for people. I just like what it says in Mark 6:34

When Jesus landed and saw the large crowd, He had compassion on them because they were like sheep without a shepherd...It is like that when I go downtown. I would be on one side of the street witnessing. I'd see so many people on the other side. I wish I could run across the street to talk with them. I never saw any christians out there witnessing, I saw Jehovah Witnesses a couple of times. I met a Prophetess downtown. She said she comes witnessing some times.

I went to one of our Malls about two months to witness. One day as I came out the restroom, I saw a security guard standing at the end of the hall. I felt he was there for me. As I got closer I heard him say into his walkie talkie, "Is this her?" So I just turned right and came home. I didn't go back to the Mall. I don't know if someone complained or if they saw me on the cameras talking to people because if they listened to me I will ask for their names and write it down to pray for them when I got home.

Some people would reject me, so instead of writing down their name, I write a number like this and still pray for them.

Ben

Alice

Couple

Mary

1,2,1,3,1,1,4,2,2,1,3 rejected

JR

James

There was so many people who rejected my witness. Some days I'd write 10 names who received my witness and 100 or more who rejected me. The rejection was always higher.

Well, get ready to be amazed, stunned and shocked at what people said about God, Jesus and the precious Holy Spirit.

Colossians 4:5 states *"Make the most of your chances to tell others the good news. Be wise in all your contact with them. Let your conversation be gracious as well as sensible, for then you will have the right answer"*. The Book

~~101~~ NO 262 REASONS WHY THE SAINTS NEED TO WITNESS!

CHAPTER 1

Did God Sin?

1 BREATHING IS A SIN:

I was in total shock to hear such a thing. Then I thought, he's old. He was my stepfather. I explained to him if breathing was a sin, God would be the biggest sinner, because He breathed breath into Adam, and every human being get their breath of life from God.

Then one day about five years later, I was out witnessing and asked a lady if she ever thought about being saved, and she said breathing was a sin. She looked to be in her 30's. So I explained to her what I told my stepfather.

This is a lie from the devil. He will do anything to keep people in their sins.

Genesis 2:7:
Then the Lord God formed a man from the dust of the ground and breathed into his nostrils the breath of life, and the man became a living being.

Isaiah 42:5:
This is what God the Lord says—the Creator of the heavens, who stretches them out, who spreads out the earth with all that springs from it, who gives breath to its people, and life to those who walk on it:

2 DID MARY SIN?:

This man said Mary sinned because she got pregnant before she got married. When I tried to explain how she got pregnant he didn't believe it.

Isaiah 7:14:
Therefore the Lord himself will give you a sign: The virgin will conceive and give birth to a son, and will call him Immanuel.

Luke 1:26-38:
In the sixth month of Elizabeth's pregnancy, God sent the angel Gabriel to Nazareth, a town in Galilee, to a virgin pledged to be married to a man named Joseph, a descendant of David. The virgin's name was Mary. The angel went to her and said, "Greetings, you who are highly favored! The Lord is with you."

Mary was greatly troubled at his words and wondered what kind of greeting this might be. But the angel said to her, "Do not be afraid, Mary; you have found favor with God. You will conceive and give birth to a son, and you are to call him Jesus. He will be great and will be called the Son of the Most High. The Lord God will give him the throne of his father David, and he will reign over Jacob's descendants forever; his kingdom will never end."

"How will this be," Mary asked the angel, "since I am a virgin?"

The angel answered, "The Holy Spirit will come on you, and the power of the Most High will overshadow you. So the holy one to be born will be called the Son of God. Even Elizabeth your relative is going to have a child in her old age, and she who was said to be unable to conceive is in her sixth month. For no word from God will ever fail."

"I am the Lord's servant," Mary answered. "May your word to me be fulfilled." Then the angel left her.

3 DID JESUS SIN?:

I can't remember why he said Jesus sinned, it's probably because He claimed to be the Son of God. And he didn't believe in the virgin birth. He believed Jesus was blaspheming.

Mark 1:9-11:
At that time Jesus came from Nazareth in Galilee and was baptized by John in the Jordan. Just as Jesus was coming up out of the water, he saw heaven being torn open and the Spirit descending on him like a dove. And a voice came from heaven: "You are my Son, whom I love; with you I am well pleased."

John 5:17-18:
In his defense Jesus said to them, "My Father is always at his work to this very day, and I too am working." For this reason they tried all the more to kill him; not only was he breaking the Sabbath, but he was even calling God his own Father, making himself equal with God.

4 JESUS IS NOT THE SON OF GOD
BUT A PROPHET:

I said I believe what the Bible says that Jesus is the Son of God.

John 1:47-50:

When Jesus saw Nathanael approaching, he said of him, "Here truly is an Israelite in whom there is no deceit." "How do you know me?" Nathanael asked. Jesus answered, "I saw you while you were still under the fig tree before Philip called you." Then Nathanael declared, "Rabbi, you are the Son of God; you are the king of Israel." Jesus said, "You believe because I told you I saw you under the fig tree. You will see greater things than that."

John 3:16-18:

For God so loved the world that he gave his one and only Son, that whoever believes in him shall not perish but have eternal life. For God did not send his Son into the world to condemn the world, but to save the world through him. Whoever believes in him is not condemned, but whoever does not believe stands condemned already because they have not believed in the name of God's one and only Son.

Matthew 8:28-29 & 31:

When he arrived at the other side in the region of the Gadarenes, two demon-possessed men coming from the tombs met him. They were so violent that no one could pass that way. "What do you want with us, Son of God?" they shouted. "Have you come here to torture us before the appointed time?"

The demons begged Jesus, "If you drive us out, send us into the herd of pigs."

Mark 1:23-24:
Just then a man in their synagogue who was possessed by an impure spirit cried out, "What do you want with us, Jesus of Nazareth? Have you come to destroy us? I know who you are— the Holy One of God!"

If the demons know Jesus is the Son of God it's a shame people don't believe Jesus is the Son of God.

5 GOD IS TOO PERFECT TO HAVE A SON. JESUS WAS AN ANGEL:

Hebrews 1:1-8 & 14:
In the past God spoke to our ancestors through the prophets at many times and in various ways, but in these last days he has spoken to us by his Son, whom he appointed heir of all things, and through whom also he made the universe. The Son is the radiance of God's glory and the exact representation of his being, sustaining all things by his powerful word. After he had provided purification for sins, he sat down at the right hand of the Majesty in heaven. So he became as much superior to the angels as the name he has inherited is superior to theirs.

For to which of the angels did God ever say, "You are my Son; today I have become your Father"? Or again, "I will be his Father, and he will be my Son"?

And again, when God brings his firstborn into the world, he says, "Let all God's angels worship him."

In speaking of the angels he says, "He makes his angels spirits, and his servants flames of fire."

But about the Son he says, "Your throne, O God, will last for ever and ever; a scepter of justice will be the scepter of your kingdom.

Are not all angels ministering spirits sent to serve those who will inherit salvation?

6 GOD WOULD HAVE TO BE MARRIED TO HAVE A SON:

I was talking with a muslim who said this. When I left him it came to me they don't believe Jesus was in heaven before He came to earth. But to say God is too perfect to have a son, or that God would have to be married to have a son is putting Him on a level with humans. God is a spirit a powerful God, who can do anything if He can make Adam why can't he make Himself a son.

John 17:1-5:
After Jesus said this, he looked toward heaven and prayed: "Father, the hour has come. Glorify your Son, that your Son may glorify you. 2 For you granted him authority over all people that he might give eternal life to all those you have given him. 3 Now this is eternal life: that they know you, the only true God, and Jesus Christ, whom you have sent. 4 I have brought you glory on earth by finishing the work you gave me to do. 5 And now, Father, glorify me in your presence with the glory I had with you before the world began.

Hebrews 10:5-7:
Therefore, when Christ came into the world, he said: "Sacrifice and offering you did not desire, but a body you prepared for me; with burnt offerings and sin offerings you were not pleased.

Then I said, 'Here I am—it is written about me in the scroll — I have come to do your will, O God.'"

7 GOD PUT SOMEONE ELSE ON THE CROSS:

Jesus took our place and died for us. There's no one on earth or in heaven who can take Jesus's place and die for Him.

Matthew 26:12:
When she poured this perfume on my body, she did it to prepare me for burial.

These are the statements Jesus made from the cross:

Luke 23:34:
Jesus said, "Father, forgive them, for they do not know what they are doing." And they divided up his clothes by casting lots.

God only has one son. Nobody else could call God Father but Jesus.

Luke 23:43:
Jesus answered him, "I tell you the truth, today you will be with me in paradise."

No one had authority to forgive the thief's sin but Jesus.

John 19: 26-27:
When Jesus saw his mother there, and the disciple whom he loved standing nearby, he said to her, "Woman, here is your son," and to the disciple, "Here is your mother." From that time on, this disciple took her into his home.

Jesus making sure His mother would be taken care of.

Matthew 27:46:
About three in the afternoon Jesus cried out in a loud voice, "Eli, Eli, lema sabachthani?" (which means "My God, my God, why have you forsaken me?").

God could not look at Jesus as He hung on the cross because all the sins of mankind were on Him.

John 19: 28:
Later, knowing that everything had now been finished, and so that Scripture would be fulfilled, Jesus said, "I am thirsty."

Jesus finished the task God gave Him to do.

Luke 23:46:
Jesus called out with a loud voice, "Father, into your hands I commit my spirit." When he had said this, he breathed his last.

Jesus committed Himself unto God. No other person could say these things except God's Son.

8 JESUS DIED OUT OF STUPIDITY:

He didn't explain why he said this. A lot of people say things and walk off before I can say anything.

Matthew 26:52-54:

Put your sword back in its place," Jesus said to him, "for all who draw the sword will die by the sword. Do you think I cannot call on my Father, and he will at once put at my disposal more than twelve legions of angels? But how then would the Scriptures be fulfilled that say it must happen in this way?"

John 10: 17-18:

The reason my Father loves me is that I lay down my life—only to take it up again. No one takes it from me, but I lay it down of my own accord. I have authority to lay it down and authority to take it up again. This command I received from my Father."

9 CHRISTIANITY KILLED JESUS:

1 Corinthians 2:8:

None of the rulers of this age understood it, for if they had, they would not have crucified the Lord of glory.

Christians weren't on the scene yet. Jesus was put to death by the High Priest, Pharisees and Sadducees and Pilate.

10 JESUS IS NOT GOD'S SON BECAUSE GOD WOULD HAVE TO HAVE SEX WITH MARY:

Just like I said in **#6,** God is not human.

11 JESUS CAN KISS MY _ _ _!:

I was downtown and came up behind this man and asked him, "Have you ever thought about being saved, giving your life to Jesus?" He said, "Jesus can kiss my _ _ _," and walked off. I was shocked but another man was coming so I asked him and he said:

12 JESUS CAN GO TO HELL!:

I said, "boy the demon from the first man jumped on him."

John 12:48:
There is a judge for the one who rejects me and does not accept my words; the very words I have spoken will condemn them at the last day.

John 15:18:
If the world hates you, keep in mind that it hated me first.

13 I BELIEVE IN GOD BUT NOT JESUS:

Many people don't believe Jesus is God's Son.

John 6:29:
Jesus answered, "The work of God is this: to believe in the one he has sent."

John 6:40:
For my Father's will is that everyone who looks to the Son and believes in him shall have eternal life, and I will raise them up at the last day.

John 14:6:
Jesus answered, "I am the way and the truth and the life. No one comes to the Father except through me.

14 DON'T BELIEVE IN GOD:

Many people don't believe in God. They say if there's a God why he let bad things happen to us. It's not God letting all bad things happen. Sin causes bad things to happen. If you live in this world you're going to have trouble if you're saved or not. It's part of life. But it's best to have God in your life when trouble comes, because He'll tell you what to do to come out of it.

I tell them God loves you even though you don't believe in Him.

Romans 14:11-12:
It is written:
"'As surely as I live,' says the Lord, every knee will bow before me; every tongue will acknowledge God.'"

So then, each of us will give an account of ourselves to God.

15 I DON'T TAKE JESUS SERIOUSLY:

2 Corinthians 5:10:
For we must all appear before the judgment seat of Christ, so that each of us may receive what is due us for the things done while in the body, whether good or bad.

Ephesians 5:1-2:
Follow God's example, therefore, as dearly loved children and walk in the way of love, just as Christ loved us and gave himself up for us as a fragrant offering and sacrifice to God.

Revelation 22:12-13:

"Look, I am coming soon! My reward is with me, and I will give to each person according to what they have done. I am the Alpha and the Omega, the First and the Last, the Beginning and the End.

I asked one young man that looked to be in his late teens or early twenties about being saved. He said, "I don't believe in God." I said, "How do you think you got here?" He said:

16 I CAME FROM MONKEYS:

I was shocked for a few seconds. I hadn't heard this one since I was in elementary school. I didn't think people believed in that anymore. I tried to explain to him that we did not come from monkeys, that there is a God and HE made us.

We were discussing this in Sunday School that schools teach this lie. Then one Monday I went to visit two people in the nursing home, and the father of one of them was talking to me about all the crime and how bad things are getting in the world. Then he said, "I believe we're going back to monkeys." I quickly said, "Oh No, we're not. We did not come from monkeys." He's in his 80's. I couldn't wait to get to Sunday School to talk about that conversation.

17 I BELIEVE IN THE BIG BANG:

What bang?

18 I BELIEVE IN EVOLUTION AND SCIENCE:

They believe that the whole universe is a progression of interrelated phenomena (an act of forming).

I was at work one day when the Spirit said go to the store. I said, "Lord, my boss don't need anything from the store." I knew He wanted me to witness to somebody. So I told my boss, "I'm going to the store." I saw a man sitting outside. I asked him about being saved. He said he don't believe in God. He believed in science and evolution. We talked a while but he did not receive my witness. As I left I thought death could be right around the corner, and God gave him a chance to believe and accept Him.

People don't realize how much God loves us to warn us before something bad happens. And that if they die and go to hell, they will see that person who witnessed or tried to tell them about God on judgement day, how they rejected Jesus then; it will be too late.

19 I DON'T BELIEVE IN SOMETHING I CAN'T SEE:

I said, "I see. Well, He talks to me."

He said, "Did He call your name?"

I said, "No but I know when he's talking to me."

He said, "That's what's wrong with people today. They get caught up in religion."

Then he said, "We have something in common."

I said, "If you're not saved, we don't have anything in common."

John 4:48:
"Unless you people see signs and wonders," Jesus told him, "you will never believe."

John 20:29:
Then Jesus told him, "Because you have seen me, you have believed; blessed are those who have not seen and yet have believed."

20 THIS LADY DON'T BELIEVE IN GOD:

I asked, "How do you think you got here?"

She said, "I came from my mother."

I asked, "How did your mother get here?"

She said, "from her mother."

I knew where she was going. I tried to explain about God but she didn't want to hear it.

Generis 2:7:
Then the Lord God formed a man from the dust of the ground and breathed into his nostrils the breath of life, and the man became a living being.

Isaiah 43:10:
...Before me no God was formed, nor will there be one after me.

Psalm 53:1
The fool says in his heart, "There is no God." They are corrupt, and their ways are vile; there is no one who does good.

21 I DON'T BELIEVE IN HEAVEN OR HELL:

This man said no one ever came from hell. I told about Lazarus was in hell and saw Abraham, a servant of God and asked him to send someone from hell to warn his brothers not to come there. But Abraham told him there was a gulf between them and no one could cross over. *Luke 16:19-30*

He said, "It sounds like Little Red Riding Hood. It's a bunch of mind control."

Psalm 14:2:
The Lord looks down from heaven on all mankind to see if there are any who understand, any who seek God.

Isaiah 66:1:
This is what the Lord says:
"Heaven is my throne, and the earth is my footstool...

Matthew 5:3:
Blessed are the poor in spirit, for theirs is the kingdom of heaven.

John 14:2-3:
My Father's house has many rooms; if that were not so, would I have told you that I am going there to prepare a place for you?

And if I go and prepare a place for you, I will come back and take you to be with me that you also may be where I am

HELL:

Psalm 9:17:
The wicked shall be turned into hell, and all the nations that forget God. KJV

Isaiah 5:14:
Therefore hell hath enlarged herself, and opened her mouth without measure: and their glory, and their multitude, and their pomp, and he that rejoiceth, shall descend into it. KJV

Matthew 5:22:
...And anyone who says, 'You fool!' will be in danger of the fire of hell.

Matthew 10:28:
Do not be afraid of those who kill the body but cannot kill the soul. Rather, be afraid of the One who can destroy both soul and body in hell.

Revelation 21:8:
But the cowardly, the unbelieving, the vile, the murderers, the sexually immoral, those who practice magic arts, the idolaters and all liars —they will be consigned to the fiery lake of burning sulfur...

I sure hate for people who don't believe in God and Jesus to end up in hell and then realize they were wrong, because it will be too late.

Hell is too hot and eternity is too long. I heard a preacher on TV say everybody is going to heaven but everybody is not going to stay in heaven. Everybody will be judged in heaven. So where we spend eternity is in our hands.

22 THIS IS HEAVEN:

I tried to explain to him that this is not heaven with all the sin and trouble on earth.

Revelation 20:1:
And I saw an angel coming down out of heaven...

Revelation 21:10:
And he carried me away in the Spirit to a mountain great and high, and showed me the Holy City, Jerusalem, coming down out of heaven from God.

23 THIS IS HELL:

This man said this because of all the troubles he's going through. But we have a chance to get our lives right with God. In hell there is no hope, no peace, no relief but torment forever and ever.

Isaiah 14:9:
Hell from beneath is moved for thee to meet thee at thy coming...
KJV

Ezekiel 31:16:
I made the nations tremble at the sound of its fall when I brought it down to the realm of the dead to be with those who go down to the pit....

24 DON'T BELIEVE THE BIBLE BECAUSE MEN WROTE IT:

I said "yes, men wrote the Bible, but God told them what to write." They wouldn't believe it if God wrote it Himself. That's their excuse for living in their sins.

The men who wrote the Bible were sinners just like us, but they chose to obey God. God uses people to reach people. There's no person who's going to teach love your enemies, forgive those who do you wrong, give to those who don't like you, except God be in their life. Because no one can live the way the Bible tells us to live on our own, we need the Holy Spirit living in us. People don't believe the Bible because they want to continue in their sins. They don't want to be corrected or rebuked. They don't want to give up their evil deeds or their ways. The Bible teaches us how to live a clean Holy Life that will bring us joy and peace. It teaches us about God, Jesus and the Holy Spirit. It also teaches us the evil schemes of the devil.

Matthew 6:15:
But if you do not forgive others their sins, your Father will not forgive your sins.

It teaches us not to nurse anger, not to take revenge, not to hate, not to steal, etc. People don't want to obey the Bible, so they use the excuse men wrote it. We have books teaching us how to cook, drive, raise kids, on marriage. God knew we would need instructions on how to live right, so He gave us the Bible:

Basic

Instructions

Before

Leaving

Earth

2 Timothy 3:15-17:

and how from infancy you have known the Holy Scriptures, which are able to make you wise for salvation through faith in Christ Jesus. All Scripture is God-breathed and is useful for teaching, rebuking, correcting and training in righteousness, so that the servant of God may be thoroughly equipped for every good work.

Hebrews 4:12-13:

For the word of God is alive and active. Sharper than any double-edged sword, it penetrates even to dividing soul and spirit, joints and marrow; it judges the thoughts and attitudes of the heart. Nothing in all creation is hidden from God's sight. Everything is uncovered and laid bare before the eyes of him to whom we must give account.

2 Peters 1:20-21:

Above all, you must understand that no prophecy of Scripture came about by the prophet's own interpretation of things. For prophecy never had its origin in the human will, but prophets, though human, spoke from God as they were carried along by the Holy Spirit.

25 THE SPIRIT IS PERVERTED. I PREACH THE TEN COMMANDMENTS:

How can the spirit be perverted when its Holy and the Spirit of God. Perverted means corrupt, morally bad. The Ten commandments along won't get us in heaven. We need the Holy Spirit.

John 14:26:
But the Advocate, the Holy Spirit, whom the Father will send in my name, will teach you all things and will remind you of everything I have said to you.

1 Corinthians 2:14:
The person without the Spirit does not accept the things that come from the Spirit of God but considers them foolishness, and cannot understand them because they are discerned only through the Spirit.

1 Timothy 6: 3-4:
If anyone teaches otherwise and does not agree to the sound instruction of our Lord Jesus Christ and to godly teaching, they are conceited and understand nothing...

26 THAT'S TOO RELIGIOUS AND SPIRITUAL:

I said that's a way of life; she said no, it's too commercial.

John 14:16-17:
And I will ask the Father, and he will give you another advocate to help you and be with you forever—the Spirit of truth. The world cannot accept him, because it neither sees him nor knows him. But you know him, for he lives with you and will be in you.

Romans 1:16-17:
For I am not ashamed of the gospel, because it is the power of God that brings salvation to everyone who believes: first to the

Jew, then to the Gentile. For in the gospel the righteousness of God is revealed—a righteousness that is by faith from first to last, just as it is written: "The righteous will live by faith."

The Holy Spirit comforts, talks, guides, leads and shows us things. He warns us.

One time I was going to South Carolina and I heard this still small voice saying, "Don't go." I went anyway and when I got on highway 95 I told the kids I smell pancakes and syrup. A few minutes later my car stopped. If I'd obeyed the Spirit that would not have happened.

Another time I was out witnessing and I heard a voice say go talk to the people on the porch of a house. I had talked to people there before, so I said Lord I've talked to them before so I was not going to go to that house. As I crossed the street I was going to go straight across, I felt the Spirit turn me toward the house. I said, "Lord you're something else." I witnessed to the people and they were not the same people I had talked to before.

Another time I was out witnessing and I saw three men sitting outside a store, so I asked them about being saved. Two of them answered and one didn't so I talked with them. About a month after that I saw them again and the Spirit told me to ask the man that didn't answer me the first time. I said, "Lord I asked him once he didn't answer." The Spirit said, "Ask him again." I did and he answered, I said, "Lord you're too much."

So what is perverted about the Spirit? He is precious, gentle and loving.

Romans 8:9:

...And if anyone does not have the Spirit of Christ, they do not belong to Christ.

Another reason why people don't believe the Bible is because they want to continue to hate.

1 John 3:15-18:

Anyone who hates a brother or sister is a murderer, and you know that no murderer has eternal life residing in him.

This is how we know what love is: Jesus Christ laid down his life for us. And we ought to lay down our lives for our brothers and sisters. If anyone has material possessions and sees a brother or sister in need but has no pity on them, how can the love of God be in that person? Dear children, let us not love with words or speech but with actions and in truth.

I had to throw this in because the Bible teaches us not to hate, but to love and forgive.

THE CREATION:

Genesis 1:

In the beginning God created the heavens and the earth. Now the earth was formless and empty, darkness was over the surface of the deep, and the Spirit of God was hovering over the waters.

And God said, "Let there be light," and there was light. God saw that the light was good, and he separated the light from the darkness. God called the light "day," and the darkness he called "night." And there was evening, and there was morning—the first day.

And God said, "Let there be a vault between the waters to separate water from water." So God made the vault and separated the water under the vault from the water above it. And it was so. God called the vault "sky." And there was evening, and there was morning —the second day.

And God said, "Let the water under the sky be gathered to one place, and let dry ground appear." And it was so. God called the dry ground "land," and the gathered waters he called "seas." And God saw that it was good.

Then God said, "Let the land produce vegetation: seed-bearing plants and trees on the land that bear fruit with seed in it, according to their various kinds." And it was so. The land produced vegetation: plants bearing seed according to their kinds and trees bearing fruit with seed in it according to their kinds. And God saw that it was good. And there was evening, and there was morning—the third day.

And God said, "Let there be lights in the vault of the sky to separate the day from the night, and let them serve as signs to mark sacred times, and days and years, and let them be lights in the vault of the sky to give light on the earth." And it was so. God made two great lights—the greater light to govern the day and the lesser light to govern the night. He also made the stars. God set them in the vault of the sky to give light on the earth, to govern the day and the night, and to separate light from darkness. And God saw that it was good. And there was evening, and there was morning—the fourth day.

And God said, "Let the water teem with living creatures, and let birds fly above the earth across the vault of the sky." So God created the great creatures of the sea and every living thing with *which the water teems and that moves about in it, according to their kinds, and every winged bird according to its kind. And God saw that it was good. God blessed them and said, "Be fruitful and increase in number and fill the water in the seas, and let the birds increase on the earth." And there was evening, and there was morning—the fifth day.*

And God said, "Let the land produce living creatures according to their kinds: the livestock, the creatures that move along the ground, and the wild animals, each according to its kind." And it was so. God made the wild animals according to their kinds, the livestock according to their kinds, and all the creatures that move along the ground according to their kinds. And God saw that it was good.

Then God said, "Let us make mankind in our image, in our likeness, so that they may rule over the fish in the sea and the birds in the sky, over the livestock and all the wild animals, and over all the creatures that move along the ground."

So God created mankind in his own image, in the image of God he created them; male and female he created them.

God blessed them and said to them, "Be fruitful and increase in number, fill the earth and subdue it. Rule over the fish in the sea and the birds in the sky and over every living creature that moves on the ground."

Then God said, "I give you every seed-bearing plant on the face of the whole earth and every tree that has fruit with seed in it. They will be yours for food. And to all the beasts of the earth and all the birds in the sky and all the creatures that move along the ground—everything that has the breath of life in it—I give every green plant for food." And it was so.

God saw all that he had made, and it was very good. And there was evening, and there was morning—the sixth day.

Genesis 2:2-3, & 7:
Thus the heavens and the earth were completed in all their vast array. By the seventh day God had finished the work he had been doing; so on the seventh day he rested from all his work. Then God blessed the seventh day and made it holy, because on it he rested from all the work of creating that he had done.

Then the Lord God formed a man from the dust of the ground and breathed into his nostrils the breath of life, and the man became a living being.

Genesis 2:19-23:
Now the Lord God had formed out of the ground all the wild animals and all the birds in the sky. He brought them to the man to see what he would name them; and whatever the man called each living creature, that was its name. So the man gave names to all the livestock, the birds in the sky and all the wild animals.

But for Adam no suitable helper was found. So the Lord God caused the man to fall into a deep sleep; and while he was sleeping, he took one of the man's ribs and then closed up the place with flesh. Then the Lord God made a woman from the rib he had taken out of the man, and he brought her to the man.

The man said,
"This is now bone of my bones and flesh of my flesh; she shall be called 'woman,' for she was taken out of man."

God is so awesome. He told us how the world was created and everything in it. For people who say they came from monkeys or any other animal, God created the monkey!

For those who believe in the big bang. How in the world can a bang cause people, animals and life to exist without a greater power behind it? Nothing existed before God. God made man in His image means we can talk and make choices. We show forth God in our action, by loving, forgiving, being kind, patient, etc.

CHAPTER 2

Different Religions

27 I'M BAPTIST:

I said, "You can be a saved Baptist."

She said, "No I don't agree with some of the things the saved people do" and walked off.

I said "OK!"

28 I AM JEW:

It was two men. One of them said Jesus was a great prophet. We have no desire to change. But for those who believe he's their Saviour. Good for them.

29 I AM A ROSITER:

I didn't get a chance to ask her what a Rositer is!

30 I AM A QUAKER:

I asked what is a Quaker? She said, "We don't sin and God gives us revelations everyday."

31 I'M WICKEN:

I asked, "What is that?" She just showed me a symbol on a chain and walked away.

32 I'M MUSLIM:

Muslims don't believe Jesus is the Son of God, but a great prophet.

33 ISLAM SAVED ME:

A man said this and walked into a store.

34 I'M JEHOVAH WITNESS:

She said, "You can't be saved while on earth." They don't believe in hell, that when you die you go back to dust. They believe that when Jesus come back to earth for the 1000 years all the dead will be resurrected. If you sin during the 1000 years you'll be judged and then you'll die and not exist, but if you sinned and was good during the 1000 years reign you won't die.

35 I'M HUMANITARIAN:

I asked what's that and she said we love everybody. I asked,

"Do you believe the Bible?" She said, "We pick what we want out the Bible."

I asked a man who said he was one what it was? He said they don't choose any religion.

36 I'M DEISISM:

I had to ask him how to spell this one. And of course I asked what it is. He said we don't believe God would intervene in our lives, that he believed in all religions. To pick one God above another would be unfair.

I said we're like little children if we're left alone we make a mess. We can't take care of ourselves without God.

37 I'M CATHOLIC:

The Catholic pray to Mary. They think Mary is in heaven interceding for them.

Romans 8:34:
...Christ Jesus who died—more than that, who was raised to life—is at the right hand of God and is also interceding for us.

There is no place in the Bible mentioned about Mary praying for anybody.

38 I GO TO THE HOUSE OF PRAYER:

I heard a CD where the preacher said Daddy Grace is the Holy Spirit. They take Jesus name out of songs and put Daddy Grace's name in place of Jesus.

Example: Daddy is the Lilly of the Valley. Daddy is the Rock. They worship him saying sweet sweet Daddy Grace. They say Jesus was for biblical times, and this is Daddy Grace and all other Bishops that come after him in that body are right.

I heard him say Daddy Grace is in heaven interceding for them. Well if God only used one man who did he use before Daddy Grace came?

1 Timothy 2:5-6
For there is one God and one mediator between God and mankind, the man Christ Jesus, 6 who gave himself as a ransom for all people...

Matthew 28:19-20:
Therefore go and make disciples of all nations, baptizing them in the name of the Father and of the Son and of the Holy Spirit, and teaching them to obey everything I have commanded you. And surely I am with you always, to the very end of the age.

Daddy Grace is not mentioned any place in the Bible. He was **just** a great man of God like Paul was. Pastor Mary Smalls said she heard Daddy Grace tell the people not to worship him to worship Jesus, after they saw the great miracles he did.

Acts 14:8-18:
In Lystra there sat a man who was lame. He had been that way from birth and had never walked. He listened to Paul as he was speaking. Paul looked directly at him, saw that he had faith to be healed and called out, "Stand up on your feet!" At that, the man jumped up and began to walk.

When the crowd saw what Paul had done, they shouted in the Lycaonian language, "The gods have come down to us in human form!" Barnabas they called Zeus, and Paul they called Hermes because he was the chief speaker. The priest of Zeus, whose temple was just outside the city, brought bulls and wreaths to the city gates because he and the crowd wanted to offer sacrifices to them.

But when the apostles Barnabas and Paul heard of this, they tore their clothes and rushed out into the crowd, shouting: "Friends, why are you doing this? We too are only human, like you. We are bringing you good news, telling you to turn from these worthless things to the living God, who made the heavens and the earth and the sea and everything in them. In the past, he let all nations go their own way. Yet he has not left himself without testimony: He has shown kindness by giving you rain from heaven and crops in their seasons; he provides you with plenty of food and fills your hearts with joy." Even with these words, they had difficulty keeping the crowd from sacrificing to them.

Daddy Grace told them not to worship him like Paul did. It would be a shame for Daddy Grace to go to heaven and his followers go to hell, because they made him their God. And the first commandment is *"You shall have no other gods before me. Exodus 20:3* They've put him before Jesus.

Another song a lady sang is "give your heart to Daddy to fight on because Daddy is with us."

They also believe that God only talks to Prophets in the House of Prayer. If you are saved God won't talk to you, so they don't hear from God, just their prophets.

39 I'M CATHOLIC, I WAS A PROTESTANT THINKING ABOUT BECOMING A JEW. I'M CONFUSED!:

I said, you need Jesus. pray and ask the Lord to save you.

John 14:6:
Jesus answered, "I am the way and the truth and the life. No one comes to the Father except through me.

40 I'M BUDDIST:

I asked, "Do you believe in Jesus?" They were a couple. They said, "No, don't want to talk about it."

41 I'M AGNOSTIC:

I don't believe in any one religion.

42 I'M RASTAFARIAN:

I asked what is that? She said it's a cross between Christian and Judaism.

There are hundreds maybe thousands more religions out there that are deceiving the people. We who are saved and living the truth need to keep thanking God for believing the truth.

John 8:31-32:
..."If you hold to my teaching, you are really my disciples. Then you will know the truth, and the truth will set you free."

John 16:13-15:

But when he, the Spirit of truth, comes, he will guide you into all the truth. He will not speak on his own; he will speak only what he hears, and he will tell you what is yet to come. He will glorify me because it is from me that he will receive what he will make known to you. All that belongs to the Father is mine. That is why I said the Spirit will receive from me what he will make known to you."

Hebrews 12:14:

Make every effort to live in peace with everyone and to be holy; without holiness no one will see the Lord.

John 3:19-21:

This is the verdict: Light has come into the world, but people loved darkness instead of light because their deeds were evil. Everyone who does evil hates the light, and will not come into the light for fear that their deeds will be exposed. But whoever lives by the truth comes into the light, so that it may be seen plainly that what they have done has been done in the sight of God.

43 I WAS SAVED. I'M IN ANOTHER RELIGION:

She disputed me down that you don't have to be saved to go to heaven. She was about the third person who told me this. I asked the Lord why do people get out the truth and turn to live a lie and He said, "Because they don't want to live right."

Galatians 1:6-7:

I am astonished that you are so quickly deserting the one who called you to live in the grace of Christ and are turning to a different gospel—which is really no gospel at all. Evidently some

*people are throwing you into confusion and are trying to pervert
the gospel of Christ.*

1 Timothy 4:1:
*The Spirit clearly says that in later times some will abandon the
faith and follow deceiving spirits and things taught by demons.*

2 Timothy 4: 3-4:
*For the time will come when people will not put up with sound
doctrine. Instead, to suit their own desires, they will gather
around them a great number of teachers to say what their
itching ears want to hear. They will turn their ears away from
the truth and turn aside to myths.*

So saints, do you see the need to get out of churches and go
witness to the world? Most of these people will not set foot in
a church, so we've got to tell them the truth that Jesus is
the answer.

1 Timothy 2:5-6:
*For there is one God and one mediator between God and
mankind, the man Christ Jesus, who gave himself as a ransom
for all people....*

2 Corinthians 4:4:
*The god of this age has blinded the minds of unbelievers, so that
they cannot see the light of the gospel that displays the glory of
Christ, who is the image of God.*

44 I'M ACHLEMEY:

I asked how to spell it and what is it? He said it's between
Christian and Scientology.

45 I'M A CONFORMED ATHEIST SINCE I WAS NINE. YOU'RE BARKING UP THE WRONG TREE:

Hebrews 12:14:

Make every effort to live in peace with everyone and to be holy; without holiness no one will see the Lord.

GOD:

Acts 17:24-31:

"The God who made the world and everything in it is the Lord of heaven and earth and does not live in temples built by human hands. And he is not served by human hands, as if he needed anything. Rather, he himself gives everyone life and breath and everything else. From one man he made all the nations, that they should inhabit the whole earth; and he marked out their appointed times in history and the boundaries of their lands. God did this so that they would seek him and perhaps reach out for him and find him, though he is not far from any one of us. 'For in him we live and move and have our being.' As some of your own poets have said, 'We are his offspring.'"

"Therefore since we are God's offspring, we should not think that the divine being is like gold or silver or stone—an image made by human design and skill. In the past God overlooked such ignorance, but now he commands all people everywhere to repent. For he has set a day when he will judge the world with justice by the man he has appointed. He has given proof of this to everyone by raising him from the dead."

Job 33:14-18:

For God does speak —now one way, now another—though no

one perceives it. In a dream, in a vision of the night, when deep sleep falls on people as they slumber in their beds, he may speak in their ears and terrify them with warnings, to turn them from wrongdoing and keep them from pride, to preserve them from the pit, their lives from perishing by the sword.

1 Timothy 6:15-16:

...God, the blessed and only Ruler, the King of kings and Lord of lords, who alone is immortal and who lives in unapproachable light, whom no one has seen or can see. To him be honor and might forever. Amen.

Isaiah 44:6-8:

"This is what the Lord says—Israel's King and Redeemer, the Lord Almighty: I am the first and I am the last; apart from me there is no God. Who then is like me? Let him proclaim it. Let him declare and lay out before me what has happened since I established my ancient people, and what is yet to come—yes, let them foretell what will come. Do not tremble, do not be afraid. Did I not proclaim this and foretell it long ago? You are my witnesses. Is there any God besides me? No, there is no other Rock; I know not one."

Habakkuk 2:18-20:

"Of what value is an idol carved by a craftsman? Or an image that teaches lies? For the one who makes it trusts in his own creation; he makes idols that cannot speak. Woe to him who says to wood, 'Come to life!' Or to lifeless stone, 'Wake up!' Can it give guidance? It is covered with gold and silver; there is no breath in it."

The Lord is in his holy temple; let all the earth be silent before him.

Psalm 115:2-12, 15:
Why do the nations say, "Where is their God?" Our God is in heaven; he does whatever pleases him. But their idols are silver and gold, made by human hands. They have mouths, but cannot speak, eyes, but cannot see. They have ears, but cannot hear, noses, but cannot smell. They have hands, but cannot feel, feet, but cannot walk, nor can they utter a sound with their throats. Those who make them will be like them, and so will all who trust in them.

All you Israelites, trust in the Lord—he is their help and shield. House of Aaron, trust in the Lord—he is their help and shield. You who fear him, trust in the Lord—he is their help and shield.

The Lord remembers us and will bless us: He will bless his people Israel, he will bless the house of Aaron,...

May you be blessed by the Lord, the Maker of heaven and earth.

Hebrews 11:6:
And without faith it is impossible to please God, because anyone who comes to him must believe that he exists and that he rewards those who earnestly seek him.

CHAPTER 3

God Knows My Heart

I was downtown one day and I was talking to someone. I can't remember if it was a man or a woman. I got so tired and my tongue even got tired. I had to sit down and stop talking for a while. So I sat on a bus bench until I got a little energy then I came home.

I went back downtown and was witnessing when it happened again. I bind the devil and prayed, and realized this was the devil attacking me. When I got home I called my Pastor and told him I believe I'm under attack. He said you are and prayed for me. The devil didn't like the fact that I was downtown reaching more people in a month than I did in a year going around town.

In one month I witnessed to 820 people downtown. I know the devil did not like that. So after the tired attack he started with my ankles. They started hurting. It slowed me down some because I would go downtown six days a week. So I anointed and prayed for my ankles. It didn't stop so I wouldn't go. Then one day I made up my mind, I'm going anyway, and it stopped hurting. Then after sometime he started with my right knee, it started hurting. I anointed it and prayed and kept on going. The devil really doesn't want me downtown because there's so many people to witness to and no one can tell me I can't witness down there.

I used to witness in Wal-Mart. Then one of the workers told me I couldn't witness in there.

Then one day I was outside a convenience store witnessing. I'd been there several times. The owner came out and told me I couldn't witness there so I left. I'd witness around the corner from the store. My main stores that I witnessed in is Kroger and Family Dollar. I would be careful not to let the manager hear me. I've witnessed to a couple of managers in Family Dollar.

A couple of people have come up to me and said I went to church after you witnessed to me, so its worth it.

Mark 16:15:
He said to them, "Go into all the world and preach the gospel to all creation.

46 IF HE WANT ME TO TALK TO PEOPLE IN TARGET ABOUT SAVING THEM THAT'S NOT MY KIND OF THING:

I asked a lady in Target, a big department store like Wal-Mart, if she ever thought about being saved, and she asked me why I asked her that. I said, "The Lord told me to ask people" and this was her answer:

47 NOT IN A KROGER:

Kroger is a grocery store. I asked this young man and he said, "Not in a Kroger. Do you go around harassing people all day long?" I said, "The Lord told me to do this." He hollered, "Don't tell me about the Lord."

Acts 1:8:
But you will receive power when the Holy Spirit comes on you; and you will be my witnesses in Jerusalem, and in all Judea and Samaria, and to the ends of the earth..

Acts 22:15:
You will be his witness to all people of what you have seen and heard.

1 Corinthians 15:58:
Therefore, my dear brothers and sisters, stand firm. Let nothing move you. Always give yourselves fully to the work of the Lord, because you know that your labor in the Lord is not in vain.

48 I'M NOT READY YET:

49 I DON'T WANT TO PLAY WITH GOD:

A lot of people gave me these two excuses. And most of them would say I have thought about being saved but I'm not ready or I don't want to play with God. None of us are ready to give up our sins or ways, but pray for God to help you to give up, because we don't know where death is. Tomorrow may be too late.

Isaiah 55:6-8
Seek the Lord while he may be found; call on him while he is near. Let the wicked forsake their ways and the unrighteous their thoughts. Let them turn to the Lord, and he will have mercy on them, and to our God, for he will freely pardon. "For

my thoughts are not your thoughts, neither are your ways my ways," declares the Lord.

Hebrews 3:7-8:

So, as the Holy Spirit says: "Today, if you hear his voice, do not harden your hearts...

50 GOD KNOWS MY HEART:

Yes, God knows our heart, that it's not right. Just because He knows your heart and you're still in your sins means you still have to be saved. When your heart changes, you will change.

Jeremiah 17:9:

The heart is deceitful above all things and beyond cure. Who can understand it?

Ezekiel 36:26-27:

I will give you a new heart and put a new spirit in you; I will remove from you your heart of stone and give you a heart of flesh. And I will put my Spirit in you and move you to follow my decrees and be careful to keep my laws.

Mark 7:20-23:

..."What comes out of a person is what defiles them. For it is from within, out of a person's heart, that evil thoughts come— sexual immorality, theft, murder, adultery, greed, malice, deceit, lewdness, envy, slander, arrogance and folly. All these evils come from inside and defile a person.".*

Isaiah 29:13:

The Lord says: "These people come near to me with their mouth and honor me with their lips, but their hearts are far from me...

51 ARE YOU SAVED, OH NO BUT I LOVE GOD:

If you love someone you want to please them and make them happy, and being saved makes God happy.

John 14:23-24:

Jesus replied, "Anyone who loves me will obey my teaching. My Father will love them, and we will come to them and make our home with them. Anyone who does not love me will not obey my teaching...

1 John 4:20:

Whoever claims to love God yet hates a brother or sister is a liar. For whoever does not love their brother and sister, whom they have seen, cannot love God, whom they have not seen.

1 John 5:3:

...this is love for God: to keep his commands. And his commands are not burdensome,...

52 I TALK TO GOD ALL THE TIME:

This man said he's 63 and he was walking and talking to God, and a lady asked him who are you talking to and he said nobody, and she said no you're talking to God. He had a beer in his hand. I told him it's not enough to talk to God. Is God listening when you're still in your sins? You need to be an example for the younger men. Talking is not enough, God said be Holy, and come out of your sins. Just about everybody pray, but are they praying for forgiveness of their sins. Are they praying for God to save them.

Isaiah 59:1-4:
Surely the arm of the Lord is not too short to save, nor his ear too dull to hear. But your iniquities have separated you from your God; your sins have hidden his face from you, so that he will not hear. For your hands are stained with blood, your fingers with guilt. Your lips have spoken falsely, and your tongue mutters wicked things. No one calls for justice; no one pleads a case with integrity. They rely on empty arguments, they utter lies; they conceive trouble and give birth to evil.

53 I THINK I AM. I JUST BOUGHT A NEW BIBLE TODAY:

Sad to think owning a Bible will make you saved, it doesn't. She walked off before I could say anything to her.

54 WHAT'S WRONG WITH YOU? DON'T YOU SEE THIS BIBLE IN MY HAND!:

This lady hollered this to me when I asked her about being saved. I didn't see the Bible in her hand and it doesn't mean you're saved because you have a Bible.

She hollered, "I am saved," in a nasty way in front of the unsaved.

I said, "You need to change that attitude."

She said, "Don't worry about my attitude."

I said, "Jesus is worried about it."

She got up from sitting at the bus stop and went and stood up against a store window. I left her alone. I repent if I was wrong to the Lord for what I said to her in front of the unsaved.

55 ONE MAN HOLLERED "I AM SAVED AND DON'T ASK ME AGAIN!":

I must have asked him before. I witnessed to a lot of people. I don't remember who I've asked. The unsaved would say you've already asked me in a nice way when I ask them twice. It's a shame the unsaved are kinder than the saved.

Galatians 5:22:
But the fruit of the Spirit is love, joy, peace, patience, kindness, goodness, faithfulness, gentleness and self control.If we're not walking in these fruits we're walking in the flesh, if we're walking in the flesh we're walking in sin.

Colossians 3:12:
Therefore, as God's chosen people, holy and dearly loved, clothe yourselves with compassion, kindness, humility, gentleness and patience.

56 WE'VE GOT AN UNDERSTANDING:

I said the only understanding Jesus has with you, is for you to repent of your sins. If you're still in your sins there is no understanding. He agreed with me, as I was leaving. I heard him tell his gay friend he needed to hear that. They both were gay.

57 MY MOTHER IS A PASTOR. JESUS AND I HAVE A GOOD UNDERSTANDING:

I said the only understanding with God is repentance. He walked off.

58 OUR PARENTS ARE TAKING CARE OF US:

These were girls about 13 or 14. I told them they've got to know Jesus for themselves. They thought their parent's salvation would save them. God calls and uses children at any age. I know a preacher who was preaching at six years old. Samuel was a small boy when God called him.

1 Samuel 2:18:
But Samuel was ministering before the Lord—a boy wearing a linen ephod.

Jeremiah 1:4-8:
The word of the Lord came to me, saying, "Before I formed you in the womb I knew you, before you were born I set you apart; I appointed you as a prophet to the nations. "

"Alas, Sovereign Lord," I said, "I do not know how to speak; I am too young." But the Lord said to me, "Do not say, 'I am too young.' You must go to everyone I send you to and say whatever I command you. Do not be afraid of them, for I am with you and will rescue you," declares the Lord.

59 IN REVELATIONS IT SAYS SATAN HAS DECEIVED THE WHOLE WORLD:

This man said no need getting saved because satan has deceived the world. That was when satan was cast out of heaven. He deceived Eve which caused sin and deception upon the world.

Revelation 12:7-9:
Then war broke out in heaven. Michael and his angels fought against the dragon, and the dragon and his angels fought back. But he was not strong enough, and they lost their place in heaven. The great dragon was hurled down—that ancient serpent called the devil, or Satan, who leads the whole world astray. He was hurled to the earth, and his angels with him.

John 3:11:
For God so loved the world that he gave his one and only Son, that whoever believes in him shall not perish but have eternal life.

60 GOD WON'T SEND ANYONE TO HELL:

61 GOD WON'T SEND ME TO HELL FOR LOVING ANOTHER WOMAN:

I said, "No God doesn't send anyone to hell. We send ourselves there when we don't obey Him, and when we continue in our sins and don't accept Jesus as our Lord and Saviour.

Numbers 14:18:

The Lord is slow to anger, abounding in love and forgiving sin and rebellion. Yet he does not leave the guilty unpunished;...

Psalm 1:6:

For the Lord watches over the way of the righteous, but the way of the wicked leads to destruction.

Proverb 11:21

Be sure of this: The wicked will not go unpunished, but those who are righteous will go free.

62 JESUS DIDN'T TEACH ABOUT GAYS:

He was in his teens and I told him what *Romans 1:26 & 27* says about gays, but he said he wasn't going by what others say in the Bible, that Jesus didn't say anything about gays. He thought it was alright to be gay. Well Jesus didn't talk about rape, child abuse, child molesting. Does that make it right because he didn't talk about them? He called his little friend and they switched off.

Leviticus 18:22:

Do not have sexual relations with a man as one does with a woman; that is detestable.

Romans 1:26-27:

Because of this, God gave them over to shameful lusts. Even their women exchanged natural sexual relations for unnatural ones. In the same way the men also abandoned natural relations with women and were inflamed with lust for one another. Men committed shameful acts with other men, and received in themselves the due penalty for their error.

63 TWO LADIES HOLDING HANDS SAID YES THEY ARE SAVED:

If you were gay and got saved, you've got to come out of that lifestyle, because it's an abomination (extremely repulsive to God). He destroyed two cities because of homosexuality.

I asked two ladies today if they ever thought about being saved. They both said they're saved and in the church. They were walking downtown hugging. For one thing they are not saved and they're in the wrong church because God's preachers preach against homosexuality.

Genesis 18:20-21:
Then the Lord said, "The outcry against Sodom and Gomorrah is so great and their sin so grievous that I will go down and see if what they have done is as bad as the outcry that has reached me. If not, I will know."

Genesis 19:1-17, 24-26:
The two angels arrived at Sodom in the evening, and Lot was sitting in the gateway of the city. When he saw them, he got up to meet them and bowed down with his face to the ground. "My lords," he said, "please turn aside to your servant's house. You can wash your feet and spend the night and then go on your way early in the morning."

"No," they answered, "we will spend the night in the square."

But he insisted so strongly that they did go with him and entered his house. He prepared a meal for them, baking bread without yeast, and they ate. Before they had gone to bed, all the men from every part of the city of Sodom—both young and old—surrounded the house. They called to Lot, "Where are the men who came to you tonight? Bring them out to us so that we can have sex with them."

Lot went outside to meet them and shut the door behind him and said, "No, my friends. Don't do this wicked thing. Look, I have two daughters who have never slept with a man. Let me bring them out to you, and you can do what you like with them. But don't do anything to these men, for they have come under the protection of my roof."

"Get out of our way," they replied. "This fellow came here as a foreigner, and now he wants to play the judge! We'll treat you worse than them." They kept bringing pressure on Lot and moved forward to break down the door.

But the men inside reached out and pulled Lot back into the house and shut the door. Then they struck the men who were at the door of the house, young and old, with blindness so that they could not find the door.

The two men said to Lot, "Do you have anyone else here—sons-in-law, sons or daughters, or anyone else in the city who belongs to you? Get them out of here, because we are going to destroy this place. The outcry to the Lord against its people is so great that he has sent us to destroy it."

So Lot went out and spoke to his sons-in-law, who were pledged to marry his daughters. He said, "Hurry and get out of this place, because the Lord is about to destroy the city!" But his sons-in-law thought he was joking.

With the coming of dawn, the angels urged Lot, saying, "Hurry! Take your wife and your two daughters who are here, or you will be swept away when the city is punished."

When he hesitated, the men grasped his hand and the hands of his wife and of his two daughters and led them safely out of the city, for the Lord was merciful to them. As soon as they had brought them out, one of them said, "Flee for your lives! Don't look back, and don't stop anywhere in the plain! Flee to the mountains or you will be swept away!"

Then the Lord rained down burning sulfur on Sodom and Gomorrah—from the Lord out of the heavens. Thus he overthrew those cities and the entire plain, destroying all those living in the cities—and also the vegetation in the land. But Lot's wife looked back, and she became a pillar of salt.

I also asked a teenager today about being saved. I told him Jesus was coming soon, he said, "Tell him I said hello." He was gay.

People take this as a joke. They don't know how serious this is. There will be no joking, laughing, or fun in hell.

I was telling a teenage girl that it's a sin to be with another girl and what the Bible says about it. She said, "I don't care what you say I'm not giving up my girlfriend."

I came up behind this person I thought was a teenage girl. He was shaped like a girl and had a long ponytail thrown over his left shoulder that he kept playing in. When I got in front of him he put the ponytail over his mouth trying to hide his beard. It was short but it was from ear to ear and he talked to me with the ponytail over his mouth. He said that God and him had a good understanding, that God gives him dreams. He quoted **Job 33:14-15:** *For God does speak—now one way, now another—though no one perceives it. In a dream, in a vision of the night, when deep sleep falls on people...*

And other scriptures he quoted. Then he said his sins are forgiven, thinking that he can continue in sin if he repented. So I told him **Romans 6:1** says...*What shall we say, then? Shall we go on sinning so that grace may increase?* He got quiet. We got interrupted. I got his name and told him to ask God to help him to give up.

The devil has people fooled thinking they can repent one time and be forgiven and continue to sin, thinking they will go to heaven. The reason Jesus came and died was to free us from sin, so that we can know God for ourselves. We can't know God in our sins. God is a holy God. He said in **Leviticus 11:44:** *I am the Lord your God; consecrate yourselves and be holy, because I am holy...*

Sanctify means to make holy, and we can't sanctify ourselves without the Holy Spirit. Holy means set apart for God, pure, godly.
They could not be Holy in the old Testament because they didn't have the Holy Spirit. They couldn't ask God to forgive them of their sins, they had to go to the high priest and he would offer up sacrifices for their sins.

Jesus was our sacrifice so now we can do what *1 Peter 1:15-16* says: *But just as he who called you is holy, so be holy in all you do; 16 for it is written: "Be holy, because I am holy."*

1 Corinthians 6:9-10:
Or do you not know that wrongdoers will not inherit the kingdom of God? Do not be deceived: Neither the sexually immoral nor idolaters nor adulterers nor men who have sex with men nor thieves nor the greedy nor drunkards nor slanderers nor swindlers will inherit the kingdom of God.

Revelation 21:8:
But the cowardly, the unbelieving, the vile, the murderers, the sexually immoral, those who practice magic arts, the idolaters and all liars—they will be consigned to the fiery lake of burning sulfur. This is the second death

The sexual immoral are those who rape, molest, gays and all kinds of vile sexual acts, those who watch pornography or act in it.

HOW HOMOSEXUALITY AND LESBIANISM STARTS:

Homosexuality is a spirit that can enter into children when they are raped or molested. Most girls are raped by their fathers or family members and it causes them to hate men so they turn to women to have a relationship with. If they are molested by a female that lesbian spirit gets in them. Sometimes it lies dormant until they get grown, but in this day and time I see a lot of teenagers that are gay. Another way they turn lesbian is playing house. Two little girls rubbing, getting on top of each other. That lesbian spirit gets in them, and the parents don't understand or know why their kids are like that.

The same with boys who have been raped. That spirit gets in them and they turn gay. Nobody is born gay. It's a sin and God created everybody male and female. There's no half and half. We've got to teach our kids not to touch kids private parts and to tell if someone touch them. We've got to know who our children are spending the night with.

One of my church members said her daughter's teacher told her that her daughter and another girl was kissing in class. Her daughter said the other girl initiated it. They were five or six. Most likely the other girl lives in a home or sees that lifestyle. I got her daughter anointed her and bind that lesbian spirit from getting in her. Then about a year later she was spending the night with one of her friends and the mother told her mother that she was on top of her daughter. I asked her was anyone in the house gay. She said the other girl's mother is. I told her don't let her go over there anymore. That spirit was trying to get her back.

You've got to talk to your kids and notice any change in their behavior and find out what caused the change. If they have been molested or raped by a family member they will be threatened. So you've got to pull it out of them in a loving and gentle way, because they're scared, hurt and confused. If a child doesn't want to be around a person, that's a sign they did something to that child. Find out, help your child and don't give up until you find out what happened. Reassure them that no one will hurt them if they tell, so the person can be punished for what they did to them. So tell them to tell you if they are shown anything, or if anything is said to them out of the way.

DON'T IGNORE ANY CHANGES IN THEIR BEHAVIOR:

Homosexuality and Lesbianism are spirits that have to be cast out. No one is born that way.

THE LOVE OF GOD:

Deuteronomy 5:28-29:

The Lord heard you when you spoke to me, and the Lord said to me, "I have heard what this people said to you. Everything they said was good. Oh, that their hearts would be inclined to fear me and keep all my commands always, so that it might go well with them and their children forever!

To fear the Lord is not to be afraid of Him like you would fear a person or animal. To fear God is to hate evil, to obey, honor, respect and love Him.

Jeremiah 29:11-12:

For I know the plans I have for you," declares the Lord, "plans to prosper you and not to harm you, plans to give you hope and a future. Then you will call on me and come and pray to me, and I will listen to you.

Jeremiah 31:3:

..."I have loved you with an everlasting love; I have drawn you with unfailing kindness.

John 3:16:

For God so loved the world that he gave his one and only Son, that whoever believes in him shall not perish but have eternal life.

Romans 5:8:

But God demonstrates his own love for us in this: While we were still sinners, Christ died for us.

I usually go downtown two times a week to just witness. One day when I got off work it was about 98 degrees. I said to myself I'm not going to witness to no one today because it's so hot, nobody would stand and listen. Then the Spirit said "Hell is hotter." So I went. That's the love of God. He does not want anybody to go to hell.

When I don't go downtown I'll ride around in my car and stop people. I'll get out and talk to them at a bus stop or on their porch. I'll stop them if they're riding a bike. Some would look at me as if I'm crazy but they don't know their soul is at stake. I've prayed to be concerned about their soul because they are not.

Sometimes when the Spirit says go out, I'll walk several blocks; He'll have someone for me to talk to. I'll talk to 10 or more people but sometimes I'll know the one He sent me to. The love of God is that He uses us in our imperfections. We have issues in our lives but God anoints us and uses us, and we are supposed to die daily to ways, habits, attitudes, etc. If we waited until we got ourselves right, the gospel would be at a stand-still because it takes years for people to get half way right. For instance, I'm an Evangelist and God has anointed me to pray. Well for years when some preachers will be preaching, I'd be saying to myself, I can bring that out better!

One night the Lord showed me the pride in my life. We had Evangelist Lacrischia Simpson preaching on the woman with an issue of blood. I didn't have pride. I received that message, but the way the Lord showed me myself was He showed me how humble she was. I repented when He showed me. I thank Him for His mercy and love for not leaving me, and not letting me have my way. If God had waited until that night to use me, I would not be witnessing to people or writing this book He told me to write. That was 6/8/12. I've been witnessing for 14 years.

~~101~~ NO 262 REASONS WHY THE SAINTS NEED TO WITNESS!

CHAPTER 4

Rejections

64 SOME SAY A SHARP NO! AND WALK OFF.

65 SOME SAY NO THANK YOU.

66 OH NO! I'M GOOD.

67 THAT'S NOT FOR ME.

68 OH MY GOODNESS!

69 YOU JUST BLOWED ME:

I used to feel bad when people rejected me, then one day the Lord said they are not rejecting you; they are rejecting me.
I was in a grocery store and asked a couple if they ever thought about getting saved. The young lady said, "I am saved." She was almost drunk. I asked her do you have the Holy Spirit? She said, you, just "blowed me" and walked off.

70 NO MAAM I'M SORRY I AM NOT A
CHRISTIAN AND I DON'T PLAN TO BE.

71 YES & NO. I'VE GOT TO GO. (Sounds Like
a Poem)

72 WHEN I GET IN TROUBLE.

73 YES, I HAVE BUT I'M GETTING READY
TO MOVE.

74 NO, I'M ACTUALLY A WITCH:

I said, well I hope you get Jesus as she walked off.

75 I'VE THOUGHT ABOUT IT A LOT BUT DON'T
WANT TO ENGAGE.

76 I'M BEYOND THAT, BELIEVE IT OR NOT.

77 NOT IN THIS LIFETIME.

78 OH NO!

79 NO THANK YOU, YOU'RE TALKING TO THE WRONG PERSON.

80 I DON'T HAVE THE TIME:

I said, "Make time."

He said, "I can't make time I'm on a mission."

81 ABSOLUTELY NOT!

82 I LIVE IN NEW YORK:

I said you can be saved in New York.

83 I BELIEVE IN IDEALS.

84 I'M FROM CANADA.

85 MY MOTHER'S SAVED. I KNOW ALL ABOUT GOD. YOU NEED TO PREACH TO THOSE WHO DON'T KNOW.

86 I HAVE DIFFERENT THINGS GOING ON IN THAT DEPARTMENT.

87 THAT'S NONE OF YOUR BUSINESS.

88 I FOUND MY GOD IN NATURE. I PRAY TO MOTHER EARTH.

89 OH, DON'T WORRY ABOUT IT.

90 NO, NO I'M NOT A CHRISTIAN. THANK YOU THOUGH.

91 THE LADY SAID, "I JUST GOT OFF WORK."

92 I DON'T WANT TO HEAR THAT.

93 I DON'T LIKE JESUS VERY MUCH.

94 I'M NOT REALLY IN THE MOOD FOR THIS.

95 WE'RE RELIGIOUS. THANK YOU.

96 NO WAY!

97 IT'S A LONG ANSWER BUT, THANK YOU.

98 I DO TO A POINT.

99 I HAVE BUT I'M NOT INTERESTED.

100 I THOUGHT ABOUT IT AND DECIDED
I'M TOO MUCH OF A SMOKER AND
I LIKE PORK.

101 NO, BUT THANK YOU FOR THE OFFER.

102 A LADY LAUGHED AND SAID THANK YOU
AND WALKED OFF.

103 IT'S COMPLICATED.

104 THE BIBLE CONTRADICTS ITSELF.

105 I DON'T WORRY ABOUT THAT ANYMORE.

106 OH GOSH I'M IN GREAT SHAPE, THANK YOU.

107 I HAVE AND I PASS. THANK YOU
VERY MUCH.

108 NO, I THINK I'M ALL SET.

109 F_ _ _ THAT!

110 NO, I CAN'T DO THAT. SORRY.

111 WE'RE FROM ANOTHER COUNTRY.

112 I'M DOOMED.

113 TRIED IT ONCE.

114 I LIKE MY SINS:

I said, "Your sins will take you to hell."

They said, "Bye."

115 WE HAVE BUT IT DIDN'T WORK OUT.

116 I'VE BEEN APPROACHED BEFORE:

I said, "It's God sending people to you."

She said, "No I think they are coming on their own."

117 I DID ABOUT 50 TIMES.

118 OH GOOD LORD!

119 OH GOD!

120 I'VE GOT TOO MUCH IN THE CARDS GOING ON.

121 WHY ARE YOU TALKING TO ME?

122 THANK YOU, I'M SPIRITUAL.

123 I DON'T WANT TO TALK ABOUT IT.

124 NOT TODAY, WE'RE ON VACATION AND WE'RE RESTING.

125 I HAVE A PRETTY GOOD LIFE SO FAR.

126 I LIKE BEING UNSAVED.

127 NOT TODAY.

128 I'M JUST WAITING ON MY WIFE:

His wife was in a store shopping.

129 I THOUGH ABOUT IT. I'D RATHER TRUST MYSELF.

130 NOPE, I'M GOING TO HELL.

131 HE WAS SUPPOSED TO COME LAST WEEK:

He was talking about the preacher who said Jesus was coming May 21, 2011.

Mark 13:22:
For false messiahs and false prophets will appear and perform signs and wonders to deceive, if possible, even the elect.

Mark 13:32:
But about that day or hour no one knows, not even the angels in heaven, nor the Son, but only the Father.

Now if Jesus said He didn't know when He was coming back and He has all power in His hands, how can man predict when Jesus is coming when Jesus doesn't know the time. If man can go through the Bible and interpret the time, then something is wrong with Jesus or the man. Well, the man proved that something is wrong with him

132 SWEETY, WE'RE ON OUR LUNCH BREAK.

133 I'VE BEEN SAVED SO MANY TIMES.:

These people would give me their remark and keep on walking.

Samuel 8:7:
...it is not you they have rejected, but they have rejected me as their king.

John 12:48:
There is a judge for the one who rejects me and does not accept my words;...

134 SATAN'S STRAIGHT UP ALL THE WAY.

135 I HAVE A STRONG GUIDANCE IN MY LIFE. I DON'T NEED HELP! I DON'T BELIEVE IN JESUS.

136 HE LOOKED AT ME, PAUSED AND SAID, "SATAN MAYBE."

137 I AM SORRY I ALREADY GAVE MY LIFE TO SATAN.

138 I DEDICATED MY LIFE TO SATAN.

139 SATAN PROMISED ME POWER, ULTIMATE POWER:

I said, "He said that to deceive you. Satan is going to hell himself."

140 SATAN RULES:

This man asked me, "Was there something on my face that says I need it?"

I said, "I ask everybody."

"He said you need to mind your own business."

He went in the light company. When he came out he said, "Satan rules."

I said, "Not in this world."

John 8:44:
You belong to your father, the devil, and you want to carry out your father's desires. He was a murderer from the beginning, not holding to the truth, for there is no truth in him. When he lies, he speaks his native language, for he is a liar and the father of lies.

Colossians 2:10:
And in Christ you have been brought to fullness. He is the head over every power and authority.

141 ONCE SAVED, ALWAYS SAVED:

I said not if you're sinning, you're not still saved. They mistake **Romans 11:29** thinking they can continue in their sins and still go to heaven.

Romans 11:29:
For God's gifts and his call are irrevocable.

This means when God gives you a gift he doesn't take it back, even if you left God you can still work in your gifts. And that's what fool people because they are sinning, but still can pray for someone and they get healed, still prophecy and still preach. But the Bible clearly says if you sin you will go to hell.

Ezekiel 18:24:
But if a righteous person turns from their righteousness and commits sin and does the same detestable things the wicked person does, will they live? None of the righteous things that person has done will be remembered. Because of the unfaithfulness they are guilty of and because of the sins they have committed, they will die.

Matthew 7:21-23:
Not everyone who says to me, 'Lord, Lord,' will enter the kingdom of heaven, but only the one who does the will of my Father who is in heaven. Many will say to me on that day, 'Lord, Lord, did we not prophesy in your name and in your name drive out demons and in your name perform many miracles?' Then I will tell them plainly, 'I never knew you. Away from me, you evildoers!'

They were sinning but still doing miracles!

142 ALL MY NEIGHBORS ARE SAVED AND SINNING:

This man said he didn't want to get saved because all his neighbors are saved but they are sinning. I told him you've got to know God for yourself. People don't realize that they are hindering the unsaved from getting saved by the ungodly way they are living. We that are saved will sin, but we are to repent and not do that sin again. **Example:** I am a caregiver. I was working for a couple. She was giving away some pocketbooks to me and I saw $5.50 in one of them. Instead of giving the money to her husband I kept it because I was broke. Well I ended up losing $55.00 a couple of days later. And the Lord let me know why I lost the $55.00. And He said I knew better. I repented and I won't do that again.

Ephesians 4:22-28:
You were taught, with regard to your former way of life, to put off your old self, which is being corrupted by its deceitful desires; to be made new in the attitude of your minds; and to put on the new self, created to be like God in true righteousness and holiness.

Therefore each of you must put off falsehood and speak truthfully to your neighbor, for we are all members of one body. "In your anger do not sin": Do not let the sun go down while you are still angry, and do not give the devil a foothold. Anyone who has been stealing must steal no longer, but must work, doing something useful with their own hands, that they may have something to share with those in need.

1 Peter 2:11-12:

Dear friends, I urge you, as foreigners and exiles, to abstain from sinful desires, which wage war against your soul. Live such good lives among the pagans that, though they accuse you of doing wrong, they may see your good deeds and glorify God on the day he visits us.

The world is watching everything we do, they are not going by what we say, but what they see. So let's be a good example for them to follow.

143 WHEN GOD IS READY FOR ME HE'LL SAVE ME:

I said He's ready now. You don't know where death is. Tomorrow may be too late. She said, something smart. The Spirit said Let it go. I didn't. I said, "I hope you don't wait too late."

She got mad! I apologized to her. She started saying I was judging her. I left her arguing to another lady about me. I repented for not obeying the Spirit.

2 Corinthians 6:1-2:

As God's co-workers we urge you not to receive God's grace in vain. For he says, "In the time of my favor I heard you, and in the day of salvation I helped you." I tell you, now is the time of God's favor, now is the day of salvation.

Hebrew 3:15:

..."Today, if you hear his voice, do not harden your hearts as you did in the rebellion."*

Many times the Spirit would tell me "Go out." I knew He meant for me to go witness, so I'd go outside and ask the Lord show me where to go sometimes. I'd turn right most of the time and left a few times. Then He started naming places. One day He said Hitch Village, which is a project. Another time He said go to 33rd Street and turn right. That led me to a young man sitting on his porch who received my witness.

One day I was going to Kroger, a grocery store, and the Spirit said Piggly Wiggly where I asked this lady if she ever thought about being saved. She said she didn't believe in God because she was having a lot of trouble with her teenage son.

I told her, "God sent me here to talk to her because He sees what you're going through and He wants you to know Him personally. He knows all about you."

I got her number and invited her to my church. She started coming with her son. She didn't stay in the church, because she wanted God to change her son right then, but God wanted to do a work in her life. She was talking down to her son saying he was no good like his father. If she'd let God change her then the son would change. God sends His saints to people to warn them. I've talked with people that said you are the second or third person that has come to me about God. So don't take it lightly God wants you to give Him your life today.

144 I WAS IN JAIL AND NOW THAT I'M OUT I'M NOT LETTING ANYONE TELL ME WHAT TO DO:

I don't know if he meant he didn't want a preacher telling him what to do or if he meant Jesus.

Deuteronomy 11:26-27:
See, I am setting before you today a blessing and a curse—the blessing if you obey the commands of the Lord your God...

1 Samuel 15:22-23:
...To obey is better than sacrifice, and to heed is better than the fat of rams. For rebellion is like the sin of divination, and arrogance like the evil of idolatry...

Hebrew 13:17:
Have confidence in your leaders and submit to their authority, because they keep watch over you as those who must give an account...

1 Peter 2:13-4:
Submit yourselves for the Lord's sake to every human authority: whether to the emperor, as the supreme authority, or to governors, who are sent by him to punish those who do wrong and to commend those who do right.

I'm in another church that has a prison ministry. Her name is Carrie Youmans. She's 90 years old, and still has a passion for the lost. She plans to open an outreach program for the homeless, drug addicts, prostitutes, etc. She has a saying: "Everything in the gutter is not gutter material." She's a trash collector. Those people you call trash she takes them.

THE POWER OF GOD:

Exodus 14:21-22:

Then Moses stretched out his hand over the sea, and all that night the Lord drove the sea back with a strong east wind and turned it into dry land. The waters were divided, and the Israelites went through the sea on dry ground, with a wall of water on their right and on their left.

Exodus 16:4:

Then the Lord said to Moses, "I will rain down bread from heaven for you...

Nehemiah 9:21:

For forty years you sustained them in the wilderness; they lacked nothing, their clothes did not wear out nor did their feet become swollen.

Psalm 147:4:

He determines the number of the stars and calls them each by name.

Psalm 139:1-4, 7-8:

You have searched me, Lord, and you know me. You know when I sit and when I rise; you perceive my thoughts from afar. You discern my going out and my lying down; you are familiar with all my ways. Before a word is on my tongue you, Lord, know it completely.

Where can I go from your Spirit? Where can I flee from your presence? If I go up to the heavens, you are there; if I make my bed in the depths, you are there.

Luke 12:7:

Indeed, the very hairs of your head are all numbered...

Acts 17:26-28:

From one man he made all the nations, that they should inhabit the whole earth; and he marked out their appointed times in history and the boundaries of their lands. God did this so that they would seek him and perhaps reach out for him and find him, though he is not far from any one of us. 'For in him we live and move and have our being.' As some of your own poets have said, 'We are his offspring.'

This is saying God determined when we were born the year, date, and place. What amazed me when I read this was the exact place where we would live. And we thought we lived where we wanted to. It's His will for us to live where we're living.

THE POWER OF GOD!

1. He sees all things
2. He knows us before and after we're born
3. He knows our thoughts
4. He knows our words
5. He knows our deeds
6. He knows our sorrows
7. He knows our needs
8. He knows our heart
9. He knows our weakness

~~101~~ NO 262 REASONS WHY THE SAINTS NEED TO WITNESS!

CHAPTER 5

God Laughs at Me When I Sin

145 GOD SENDS MESSENGERS TO PEOPLE TO GIVE ME CIGARETTES. HE WORKS IN MYSTERIOUS WAYS:

I could tell she didn't know the truth. God doesn't give us anything to hurt us. He sends messengers to help us, warn us or bless us.

Haggai 1:13:
Then Haggai, the Lord's messenger, gave this message of the Lord to the people: "I am with you," declares the Lord.

Malachi 3:1:
"I will send my messenger, who will prepare the way before me...

Acts 11:13-14:
He told us how he had seen an angel appear in his house and say, 'Send to Joppa for Simon who is called Peter. He will bring

you a message through which you and all your household will be saved.'

146 YES I AM SAVED. HE'S IN FRONT OF ME LAUGHING WHEN I DO WRONG:

God does not laugh at us when we sin. He hates sin. What's funny about sin?

Psalm 59:8:
But you laugh at them, Lord; you scoff at all those nations.

Psalm 37:13:
But the Lord laughs at the wicked, for he knows their day is coming.

Proverb 1:24-26:
But since you refuse to listen when I call and no one pays attention when I stretch out my hand, since you disregard all my advice and do not accept my rebuke, I in turn will laugh when disaster strikes you; I will mock when calamity overtakes you—

147 MAN LEFT OUT 16 BOOKS OF THE BIBLE. THEY LEFT OUT ENOCH, THE LARGEST BOOK. GOD DID NOT GIVE JESUS POWER, HE GAVE BLACK WOMEN POWER. MEN BOWED DOWN TO THEM:

I don't know what planet he came from. He did all the talking. I could hardly get a word in. But I did tell him the books in the Bible is just what we need.

Matthew 28:18:
Then Jesus came to them and said, "All authority in heaven and on earth has been given to me.

John 3:35-36:
The Father loves the Son and has placed everything in his hands. Whoever believes in the Son has eternal life, but whoever rejects the Son will not see life, for God's wrath remains on them.

148 OUR SINS ARE ALREADY FORGIVEN. WE'RE THE REINCARNATED JEWS. WE DIDN'T COME OVER ON SLAVE SHIPS:

Acts 2:38:
Peter replied, "Repent and be baptized, every one of you, in the name of Jesus Christ for the forgiveness of your sins. And you will receive the gift of the Holy Spirit.

Galatians 3:26-28:
So in Christ Jesus you are all children of God through faith, for all of you who were baptized into Christ have clothed yourselves with Christ. There is neither Jew nor Gentile, neither slave nor free, nor is there male and female, for you are all one in Christ Jesus.

There is no such thing as reincarnation. Once you die you do not come back to earth. Your soul will be either in heaven if you repent of your sin before you die, or in hell if you don't repent of your sin. The blacks are not reincarnated Jews, for God doesn't show favoritism to one race over others. We who are saved are adopted whether black, white, Mexican, Greek, Indian etc.

149 I BELIEVE THERE ARE A BUNCH OF LITTLE GODS UP THERE, THE HINDUS, BUDDHA ETC. I DON'T PUT ONE GOD ABOVE THE OTHER:

Isaiah 43:10:
...Before me no god was formed, nor will there be one after me.

Isaiah 45: 5&7:
I am the Lord, and there is no other; apart from me there is no God...

I form the light and create darkness, I bring prosperity and create disaster; I, the Lord, do all these things.

150 I SERVE NO MAN:

This lady said her god's name was "no man". I told her I was working for the Lord. She asked me how much was Jesus paying me. I said, "He doesn't pay me money for witnessing." She said, "I'll tell 'no man' to tell Jesus to pay you for working for him."

John 4:34-36:
"My food," said Jesus, "is to do the will of him who sent me and to finish his work.

...open your eyes and look at the fields! They are ripe for harvest.

Even now the one who reaps draws a wage and harvests a crop for eternal life,...

1 Corinthians 3:8:
The one who plants and the one who waters have one purpose, and they will each be rewarded according to their own labor.

1 Corinthians 15:58
Therefore, my dear brothers and sisters, stand firm. Let nothing move you. Always give yourselves fully to the work of the Lord, because you know that your labor in the Lord is not in vain.

151 I TRIED JESUS SEVERAL TIMES. I CHOOSE DARKNESS TO SAVE ME:

I said nobody can save you but Jesus. If we don't accept Him we send ourself to hell.

She said, "Hell is near Syria."

Then she said, "When I see you in hell I'll wave at you."

I quickly said, "Oh no, you won't see me there."

Luke 16:23-24:
In Hades, where he was in torment...

...'Father Abraham, have pity on me and send Lazarus to dip the tip of his finger in water and cool my tongue, because I am in agony in this fire.'

John 3:19-20:
This is the verdict: Light has come into the world, but people loved darkness instead of light because their deeds were evil. Everyone who does evil hates the light, and will not come into the light for fear that their deeds will be exposed.

Acts 4:12:

Salvation is found in no one else, for there is no other name under heaven given to mankind by which we must be saved.

152 GOD GAVE MY COUSIN TYRONE TO DIE FOR US:

She said God was with her before Christianity, before Judaism, that he gave her cousin Tyrone to die for us.

Jesus is the only one that died for us. He's the only one that can save us.

John 14:6:

Jesus answered, "I am the way and the truth and the life. No one comes to the Father except through me.

Matthew 16:21:

...Jesus began to explain to his disciples that he must go to Jerusalem and suffer many things at the hands of the elders, the chief priests and the teachers of the law, and that he must be killed and on the third day be raised to life.

1 Timothy 2:5-6:

For there is one God and one mediator between God and mankind, the man Christ Jesus, 6 who gave himself as a ransom for all people...

153 I BELIEVE IF HE WANTS ME TO GIVE MY LIFE TO HIM, HE WOULDN'T HAVE TAKEN A LIFE FROM ME:

I tried to tell him that people die. We're not going to live here forever, but he walked off.

Ecclesiastes 3:1-2:
There is a time for everything, and a season for every activity under the heavens:

a time to be born and a time to die...

Psalm 49:7-9:
No one can redeem the life of another or give to God a ransom for them—the ransom for a life is costly, no payment is ever enough—so that they should live on forever and not see decay.

154 I THINK JESUS WAS AN ALIEN WITH HUMAN FORM, BUT I THINK IT'S INTERESTING. AND HE KEPT ON WALKING:

John 1:29:
The next day John saw Jesus coming toward him and said, "Look, the Lamb of God, who takes away the sin of the world!"

Revelation 5:6-9:
Then I saw a Lamb, looking as if it had been slain, standing at the center of the throne...He went and took the scroll from the right hand of him who sat on the throne...the four living creatures and the twenty-four elders fell down before the

Lamb...And they sang a new song, saying: "You are worthy to take the scroll and to open its seals, because you were slain, and with your blood you purchased for God persons from every tribe and language and people and nation.

155 I BELIEVE IN FIRE AND WATER:

God created fire and water. Fire burns you, water drowns you so how can fire and water save you?

Genesis 1:9:
And God said, "Let the water under the sky be gathered to one place, and let dry ground appear." And it was so

Exodus 3:1-4:
Now Moses was tending the flock of Jethro his father-in-law, the priest of Midian, and he led the flock to the far side of the wilderness and came to Horeb, the mountain of God. There the angel of the Lord appeared to him in flames of fire from within a bush. Moses saw that though the bush was on fire it did not burn up. So Moses thought, "I will go over and see this strange sight—why the bush does not burn up."

When the Lord saw that he had gone over to look, God called to him from within the bush, "Moses! Moses!"

And Moses said, "Here I am."

God is speaking through the fire.

WHAT GOD HATES:

Proverbs 6:16-19:

There are six things the Lord hates, seven that are detestable to him: haughty eyes, a lying tongue, hands that shed innocent blood, a heart that devises wicked schemes, feet that are quick to rush into evil, a false witness who pours out lies and a person who stirs up conflict in the community.

Proverbs 11:1:

The Lord detests dishonest scales, but accurate weights find favor with him.

Proverbs 15:8-10:

The Lord detests the sacrifice of the wicked...The Lord detests the way of the wicked,but he loves those who pursue righteousness.

Stern discipline awaits anyone who leaves the path; the one who hates correction will die.

Proverbs 17:5:

Whoever mocks the poor shows contempt for their Maker; whoever gloats over disaster will not go unpunished.

Proverbs 18:3:

When wickedness comes, so does contempt, and with shame comes reproach.

Proverbs 22:22-23:

Do not exploit the poor because they are poor and do not crush the needy in court, for the Lord will take up their case and will exact life for life.

Proverbs 24:19-20:

Do not fret because of evildoers or be envious of the wicked, for the evildoer has no future hope, and the lamp of the wicked will be snuffed out.

Malachi 21:16

For the Lord, the God of Israel, says He hates divorce and cruel men. Therefore control your passion–Let there be no divorcing of your wives or husbands–The Book

CHAPTER 6

The Deceptions of Satan

156 MILLIONS OF TIMES I CHOSE OBAMA TO SAVE ME:

She walked into a store before I could say anything.

Psalm 146:3-5:

Do not put your trust in princes, in human beings, who cannot save. When their spirit departs, they return to the ground; on that very day their plans come to nothing. Blessed are those whose help is the God of Jacob, whose hope is in the Lord their God.

Proverbs 3:5-6:

Trust in the Lord with all your heart and lean not on your own understanding; in all your ways submit to him, and he will make your paths straight.

157 I LOOKED INTO MY SOUL AND REALIZED I DON'T NEED IT:

When I thought I'd heard the wildest thing, then someone would come up with something wilder.

1 Corinthians 1:18-19:

For the message of the cross is foolishness to those who are perishing, but to us who are being saved it is the power of God.

For it is written: "I will destroy the wisdom of the wise; the intelligence of the intelligent I will frustrate."

158 I WAS BORN SAVED:

I said only Jesus, John the Baptist and Jeremiah were born saved. Another Lady said, "No!" and kept on walking. When she got a half block from me she turned around and hollered, "I was saved when I was born." I hollered back, "No you weren't."

Psalm 51:5

Surely I was sinful at birth, sinful from the time my mother conceived me.

Romans 3:23:

For all have sinned and fall short of the glory of God.

159 I SAVED MYSELF. YOU CAN CHOOSE WHO YOU WANT TO SAVE YOU:

Acts 4:12:

Salvation is found in no one else, for there is no other name under heaven given to mankind by which we must be saved.

This is why we've got to get out the churches and into the streets to tell people the truth. Many will never set foot in church, and they are believing lies.

160 I'M SAVED IN MY OWN WAY:

There's only one way to be saved and that's through Jesus.

John 14:6

Jesus answered, "I am the way and the truth and the life. No one comes to the Father except through me.

John 3:17:

For God did not send his Son into the world to condemn the world, but to save the world through him.

161 I DETERMINE WHAT HAPPENS TO ME WHEN I DIE:

Ecclesiastes 8:8:

As no one has power over the wind to contain it, so no one has power over the time of their death...

Job 14:10:

But a man dies and is laid low; he breathes his last and is no more.

Luke 12:5:
...Fear him who, after your body has been killed, has authority to throw you into hell...

162 I HAVE A LIFE STYLE PLAN FOR ME.

163 I'VE GOT A LIFE AHEAD OF ME:

We don't know where death is. Babies, children, teenagers, and the elderly are dying everyday. Tomorrow may be too late.

Psalm 34:11-17:
Come, my children, listen to me; I will teach you the fear of the Lord. Whoever of you loves life and desires to see many good days, keep your tongue from evil and your lips from telling lies. Turn from evil and do good; seek peace and pursue it.

The eyes of the Lord are on the righteous, and his ears are attentive to their cry; but the face of the Lord is against those who do evil, to blot out their name from the earth.

The righteous cry out, and the Lord hears them; he delivers them from all their troubles.

Proverb 3:5-8:
Trust in the Lord with all your heart and lean not on your own understanding; in all your ways submit to him, and he will make your paths straight.

Do not be wise in your own eyes; fear the Lord and shun evil. This will bring health to your body and nourishment to your bones.

Luke 12:16-20:

And he told them this parable: "The ground of a certain rich man yielded an abundant harvest. He thought to himself, 'What shall I do? I have no place to store my crops.'

"Then he said, 'This is what I'll do. I will tear down my barns and build bigger ones, and there I will store my surplus grain. And I'll say to myself, "You have plenty of grain laid up for many years. Take life easy; eat, drink and be merry."'

"But God said to him, 'You fool! This very night your life will be demanded from you. Then who will get what you have prepared for yourself?'

164 I DON'T NEED SAVING FROM ANYTHING.

165 I HAVEN'T BEEN LOST YET.

166 I NEVER THOUGHT I WAS LOST:

Matthew 18:11:
The Son of Man came to save what was lost.

Luke 19:9-10:
Jesus said to him, "Today salvation has come to this house, because this man, too, is a son of Abraham. For the Son of Man came to seek and to save the lost."

Lost: to no longer possess, beyond reach, ruined, physically or morally lacking eternal salvation.

167 WHAT SINS HAVE I DONE?:

You sinned if you lied, thought evil, hated, had pride, unforgiveness, or gossiped.

Psalm 51:5:
Surely I was sinful at birth, sinful from the time my mother conceived me.

Proverbs 20:9:
Who can say, "I have kept my heart pure; I am clean and without sin"?

Romans 3:23:
For all have sinned and fall short of the glory of God.

1 John 1:8:
If we claim to be without sin, we deceive ourselves and the truth is not in us.

168 WHY SHOULD I WANT TO GIVE UP MY SINS?:

One lady asked me this and kept on walking.

Romans 6:23:
For the wages of sin is death, but the gift of God is eternal life in Christ Jesus our Lord.

169 WHAT IS SIN?

This lady asked, "What is sin?"

Sin is breaking the Laws of God. The act of not doing what God wants.

1 John 5:17:
All wrongdoing is sin...

1. disobedience
2. drunkeness
3. thinking evil
4. fornication - sex outside of marriage
   I had a friend in her 40's who did not know this was a sin.
5. stealing
6. hatred
7. taking bribes
8. despising your husband or wife
9. pride
10. lying - little white lies
11. incest
12. sodomy
13. homosexual
14. Lesbian
15. rape
16. unthankful
17. cursing
18. denying Jesus
19. hypocrisy
20. causing division
21. murder
22. rebellion
23. covetousness
24. compromise
25. practicing witchcraft
26. horoscope

27. fortune telling
28. gossip
29. jealousy
30. racism
31. child abuse

170 I HAVEN'T BEEN BORN YET:

This lady said she doesn't believe in God, I said, "He loves you though you don't believe in Him." Then she said, "I haven't been born yet." and walked off. I was stunned of course.

171 I'M SAVED BUT I DON'T GO TO CHURCH

I tell them they need to go to church to be in the anointing and to be revived, to be strengthened. The longer you stay out the weaker you get. If Jesus went to church which was called the synagogue, how much more are we to go.

Luke 4:16:
He went to Nazareth, where he had been brought up, and on the Sabbath day he went into the synagogue, as was his custom. He stood up to read...

Acts 2:42:
They devoted themselves to the apostles' teaching and to fellowship, to the breaking of bread and to prayer.

Hebrews 10:25:
...not giving up meeting together, as some are in the habit of

doing, but encouraging one another—and all the more as you see the Day approaching.

172 I TEACH MYSELF. I'M TRYING TO LIVE SAVED:

No one can teach themselves how to live a saved life. You've got to go to church to hear the word of God. You've got to be taught how to give up your ways, how to give up your sins, and how to deny yourself, how to fight the devil.

Romans 10:14:
...And how can they hear without someone preaching to them?

173 I BACKSLIDE:

Ask the Lord to help you to give up. He said, "We've got a little stand-off going."

174 GOD IS MARRIED TO THE BACKSLIDER:

She was drinking and was using this as an excuse. She said she was still going to heaven.

Joel 2:12-13:
"Even now," declares the Lord, "Return to me with all your heart, with fasting and weeping and mourning."

Rend your heart and not your garments. Return to the Lord your God, for he is gracious and compassionate, slow to anger and abounding in love, and he relents from sending calamity.

Jeremiah 3:14-15:
"Return, faithless people," declares the Lord, "for I am your husband. I will choose you—..Then I will give you shepherds after my own heart, who will lead you with knowledge and understanding.

175 I'M SAVED BUT YOU OFFEND ME BY ASKING ME THAT:

More people who said they are saved get offended more than the unsaved do, and they answer so rude and mean. I told one lady she needed more saving. She was talking so mean.

176 ONE LADY GOT MAD AND SAID, "LET ME ASK YOU, WHY WOULD YOU ASK ME THAT? IT'S OFFENSIVE AND AN INTRUSION OF PRIVACY":

She said she'd been all around the world. I said I asked people about being saved, she started arguing. I left her alone.

Matthew 11:6:
And blessed is he, whosoever shall not be offended in me.

1 Corinthians 1:18:
For the preaching of the cross is to them that perish foolishness, but unto us which are saved it is the power of God.

177 ONE LADY SAID SHE'S SAVED. I SAID, "YOU'VE GOT TO STOP CURSING:"

I said, "You're doing the same thing the unsaved do. You're not being a light."

She said, "They're not to do what they see us do."

I said, "You're hindering them from being saved because they don't see a difference between you and them."

She started arguing, so I left.

Some people think when they join the church and get baptized, they're saved. They don't repent, their life doesn't change. They continue doing what they've been doing–cursing, drinking, living like the devil, and they think they are saved.

Ephesians 4:29:
Do not let any unwholesome talk come out of your mouths, but only what is helpful for building others up according to their needs, that it may benefit those who listen.

James 3:9-11:
With the tongue we praise our Lord and Father, and with it we curse human beings, who have been made in God's likeness. Out of the same mouth come praise and cursing. My brothers and sisters, this should not be. Can both fresh water and salt water flow from the same spring?

JESUS:

John 6:38-39:

For I have come down from heaven not to do my will but to do the will of him who sent me. And this is the will of him who sent me, that I shall lose none of all those he has given me, but raise them up at the last day.

John 10:10-11 & 17-18:

The thief comes only to steal and kill and destroy; I have come that they may have life, and have it to the full. "I am the good shepherd. The good shepherd lays down his life for the sheep.

The reason my Father loves me is that I lay down my life—only to take it up again. No one takes it from me, but I lay it down of my own accord. I have authority to lay it down and authority to take it up again. This command I received from my Father."

John 12:44-47:

Then Jesus cried out, "Whoever believes in me does not believe in me only, but in the one who sent me. The one who looks at me is seeing the one who sent me. I have come into the world as a light, so that no one who believes in me should stay in darkness. "If anyone hears my words but does not keep them, I do not judge that person. For I did not come to judge the world, but to save the world.

John 14:1-3:

"Do not let your hearts be troubled. You believe in God; believe also in me. My Father's house has many rooms; if that were not so, would I have told you that I am going there to prepare a place for you? And if I go and prepare a place for you, I will

come back and take you to be with me that you also may be where I am.

Acts 1:9-11

After he said this, he was taken up before their very eyes, and a cloud hid him from their sight. They were looking intently up into the sky as he was going, when suddenly two men dressed in white stood beside them. "Men of Galilee," they said, "why do you stand here looking into the sky? This same Jesus, who has been taken from you into heaven, will come back in the same way you have seen him go into heaven."

Philippians 2:5-11:

In your relationships with one another, have the same mindset as Christ Jesus: Who, being in very nature God, did not consider equality with God something to be used to his own advantage; rather, he made himself nothing by taking the very nature of a servant, being made in human likeness. And being found in appearance as a man, he humbled himself by becoming obedient to death—even death on a cross! Therefore God exalted him to the highest place and gave him the name that is above every name, that at the name of Jesus every knee should bow, in heaven and on earth and under the earth, and every tongue acknowledge that Jesus Christ is Lord, to the glory of God the Father.

John 3:35-36:

The Father loves the Son and has placed everything in his hands. Whoever believes in the Son has eternal life, but whoever rejects the Son will not see life, for God's wrath remains on them.

Hebrews 7:24-25:
But because Jesus lives forever, he has a permanent priesthood.
Therefore he is able to save completely those who come to God
through him, because he always lives to intercede for them.

Hebrews 9:27-28:
Just as people are destined to die once, and after that to face
judgment, so Christ was sacrificed once to take away the sins of
many; and he will appear a second time, not to bear sin, but to
bring salvation to those who are waiting for him.

The Catholics says Mary is interceding (praying to God) for
them. The House of Prayer says Daddy Grace is in heaven
interceding for them, so where is Jesus? **Hebrews 13:8** says
Jesus Christ is the same yesterday and today and forever. So that
means He did not leave the right hand of God, He did not get
up from His throne at the right hand of God, to let Mary or
Daddy Grace take His place praying for us.

Hebrews 10:5-7:
Therefore, when Christ came into the world, he said:"Sacrifice
and offering you did not desire, but a body you prepared for me;
with burnt offerings and sin offerings you were not pleased.
Then I said, 'Here I am—it is written about me in the scroll—I
have come to do your will, my God.'"

Why give more praise to people who accepted Jesus as their
Savior? Mary and Daddy Grace and others that people have
put above Jesus, got saved through Jesus!

CHAPTER 7

I have My Spirit

178 DO YOU HAVE THE HOLY SPIRIT? "I HAVE MY SPIRIT":

I asked people this when they say they're saved. Some people say I don't know about that, some say I think I do. This man said I have my spirit, then I know they don't have the Holy Spirit. So I tell them the Holy Spirit is the Spirit of God, the power of God that lives in us, that keeps us saved. And we need the Holy Spirit so we'll be able to rise when Jesus comes back in the rapture. It's like a magnet that will draw us up to meet Jesus in the sky. And those who don't have the Holy Spirit won't rise because there won't be any connection.

1 Corinthians 6:19-20:

...your bodies are temples of the Holy Spirit...whom you have received from God? You are not your own; you were bought at a price. Therefore honor God with your bodies.

John 14:16-17:

And I will ask the Father, and he will give you another advocate to help you and be with you forever—the Spirit of truth. The world cannot accept him, because it neither sees him nor knows him. But you know him, for he lives with you and will be in you.

179 I DID ROMANS 10:9:

If you declare with your mouth, "Jesus is Lord," and believe in your heart that God raised him from the dead, you will be saved.

A lot of men told me they did **Romans 10:9** when they were in jail. And when they get out they don't change their life. They're still sinning and doing the things that sent them to jail. They think by confessing this verse they are saved, but when you confess this verse, you're to repent of your sins, and not continue sinning.

Romans 6:1-2:
What shall we say, then? Shall we go on sinning so that grace may increase? By no means! We are those who have died to sin; how can we live in it any longer?

Romans 6:11-14, 16, 19:
In the same way, count yourselves dead to sin but alive to God in Christ Jesus. Therefore do not let sin reign in your mortal body so that you obey its evil desires. Do not offer any part of yourself to sin as an instrument of wickedness, but rather offer yourselves to God as those who have been brought from death to life; and offer every part of yourself to him as an instrument of righteousness. For sin shall no longer be your master...

Don't you know that when you offer yourselves to someone as obedient slaves, you are slaves of the one you obey—whether you are slaves to sin, which leads to death, or to obedience, which leads to righteousness?

...Just as you used to offer yourselves as slaves to impurity and to ever-increasing wickedness, so now offer yourselves as slaves to righteousness leading to holiness.

2 Timothy 2:19:
Nevertheless, God's solid foundation stands firm, sealed with this inscription: "The Lord knows those who are his," and, "Everyone who confesses the name of the Lord must turn away from wickedness."

180 I'M A CHRISTIAN:

A lot of people think that because they joined the church and got baptized that they are a Christian. A Christian is anyone who has the Spirit of God living in them. If you have repented of your sins, and living according to what the Bible tells us to do, if it says do something do it.

Example: Pray for your enemy. You can't do this on your own so you've got to ask God to help you to forgive them so you can pray for them.

Matthew 5:43-44:
"You have heard that it was said, 'Love your neighbor and hate your enemy.' But I tell you, love your enemies and pray for those who persecute you, that you may be children of your Father in heaven...

The Bible tells us what not to do. **Do not commit adultery.**

Matthew 5:27-28:
"You have heard that it was said, 'You shall not commit adultery.' But I tell you that anyone who looks at a woman lustfully has already committed adultery with her in his heart.

Ephesians 5:18:
Do not get drunk on wine, which leads to wild living. Instead, be filled with the Spirit.

Romans 8:9:
...And if anyone does not have the Spirit of Christ, they do not belong to Christ.

When the Holy Spirit comes in our life then we are Christians. The Holy Spirit is the Spirit of God which helps you to live a saved life. Your thinking changes, your talk changes, you don't gossip, you don't back bite, you don't do the things you use to do or go the places you used to go. Your heart changes. You really fall in love with God from your heart, and you'll want to make him happy. A lot of people say they love God, but they don't obey Him. When you continue in your sins you do not love God, and you are not a Christian. Just because you were born in the church, sing in the choir all your life, usher all your life, even preach, doesn't mean you are a christian. Christian means Christ-like Is your life similar to Jesus?. He was our example when He was on earth. Are you doing what Jesus did? Are you loving like He did? Are you forgiving like He did? Are you humble like He was?

Are you doing what **Romans 12:14-21** says? *Bless those who persecute you; bless and do not curse. Rejoice with those who rejoice; mourn with those who mourn. Live in harmony with* *one another. Do not be proud, but be willing to associate with people of low position. Do not be conceited. Do not repay anyone evil for evil. Be careful to do what is right in the eyes of everyone. If it is possible, as far as it depends on you, live at peace with everyone. Do not take revenge, my dear friends, but leave room for God's wrath, for it is written: "It is mine to avenge; I will repay," says the Lord. On the contrary: "If your enemy is hungry, feed him; if he is thirsty, give him something to drink. In doing this, you will heap burning coals on his head." Do not be overcome by evil, but overcome evil with good.*

Romans 13:9-10:
The commandments, "You shall not commit adultery," "You shall not murder," "You shall not steal," "You shall not covet," and whatever other command there may be, are summed up in this one command: "Love your neighbor as yourself." Love does no harm to a neighbor. Therefore love is the fulfillment of the law.

Romans 13:14:
Rather, clothe yourselves with the Lord Jesus Christ, and do not think about how to gratify the desires of the flesh.

181 THE BIBLE SAYS DON'T JUDGE:

This man said he was saved and he was sending someone to get him some beer and cigarettes. People don't realize when you're saved your life has to change. How can you be a witness to people when you're doing the same thing they're doing?

I was talking to a Baptist Preacher one day about drinking; he said it was alright to drink as long as you don't get drunk. So I said if an alcoholic gets saved and you tell him it's alright to drink, just don't get drunk, there's no way he can drink one or two drinks without drinking more and getting drunk. I asked the Lord about it and He said people drink because they want to.

Proverbs 20:1:

Wine is a mocker and beer a brawler; whoever is led astray by them is not wise.

Proverbs 31:4-7:

It is not for kings, Lemuel—it is not for kings to drink wine, not for rulers to crave beer, lest they drink and forget what has been decreed, and deprive all the oppressed of their rights. Let beer be for those who are perishing, wine for those who are in anguish! Let them drink and forget their poverty and remember their misery no more.

Isaiah 5:11-12:

Woe to those who rise early in the morning to run after their drinks, who stay up late at night till they are inflamed with wine. They have harps and lyres at their banquets, pipes and timbrels and wine, but they have no regard for the deeds of the Lord, no respect for the work of his hands.

Isaiah 5:22:

Woe to those who are heroes at drinking wine and champions at mixing drinks

Ephesians 5:18-19:

Do not get drunk on wine, which leads to wild living. Instead, be filled with the Spirit, speaking to one another with psalms, hymns, and songs from the Spirit. Sing and make music from your heart to the Lord

1 Timothy 5:23:
Stop drinking only water, and use a little wine because of your stomach and your frequent illnesses.

Paul was telling Timothy to use wine as a medicine. There is a non-alcoholic wine in stores.

There's a lot of saints who still smoke. When I see them, I tell them the story I heard Joyce Meyers told of how she stopped smoking. She said every time she took a puff she would say "Thank God I don't smoke any more," until she stopped.

About a year ago a man came up to me and said, "I'm doing what you said and I've cut back" and another man came up to me two days ago and said, "I did what you told me and I don't smoke anymore." We were at a bus stop. I always go to different bus stops downtown and witness.

A lady said she was saved and I told her that I told the man to say "Thank God I don't smoke anymore." It was meant for her to hear that because she wanted to quit smoking. I was thinking that works for people who want to stop smoking. If people want to stop drinking say, "Thank God I don't drink anymore" every time they take a drink and see what happens.

Proverbs 18:21:
The tongue has the power of life and death, and those who love it will eat its fruit.

182 I'VE DONE TOO MUCH SIN:

One man told me this and I told him that's a lie from the devil to keep you in your sins.

I didn't know how I was going to answer this one from the Bible, but thank God He let me come across the answer one day while reading the Bible. This let's me know that the Bible has an answer for every problem in life.

1 King 21:

Some time later there was an incident involving a vineyard belonging to Naboth the Jezreelite. The vineyard was in Jezreel, close to the palace of Ahab king of Samaria. Ahab said to Naboth, "Let me have your vineyard to use for a vegetable garden, since it is close to my palace. In exchange I will give you a better vineyard or, if you prefer, I will pay you whatever it is worth."

But Naboth replied, "The Lord forbid that I should give you the inheritance of my ancestors."

So Ahab went home, sullen and angry because Naboth the Jezreelite had said, "I will not give you the inheritance of my ancestors." He lay on his bed sulking and refused to eat.

His wife Jezebel came in and asked him, "Why are you so sullen? Why won't you eat?"

He answered her, "Because I said to Naboth the Jezreelite, 'Sell me your vineyard; or if you prefer, I will give you another vineyard in its place.' But he said, 'I will not give you my vineyard.'"

Jezebel his wife said, "Is this how you act as king over Israel? Get up and eat! Cheer up. I'll get you the vineyard of Naboth the Jezreelite."

So she wrote letters in Ahab's name, placed his seal on them, and sent them to the elders and nobles who lived in Naboth's city with him. In those letters she wrote:

"Proclaim a day of fasting and seat Naboth in a prominent place among the people. But seat two scoundrels opposite him and have them bring charges that he has cursed both God and the king. Then take him out and stone him to death."

So the elders and nobles who lived in Naboth's city did as Jezebel directed in the letters she had written to them. They proclaimed a fast and seated Naboth in a prominent place among the people. Then two scoundrels came and sat opposite him and brought charges against Naboth before the people, saying, "Naboth has cursed both God and the king." So they took him outside the city and stoned him to death. Then they sent word to Jezebel: "Naboth has been stoned to death."

As soon as Jezebel heard that Naboth had been stoned to death, she said to Ahab, "Get up and take possession of the vineyard of Naboth the Jezreelite that he refused to sell you. He is no longer alive, but dead." When Ahab heard that Naboth was dead, he got up and went down to take possession of Naboth's vineyard.

Then the word of the Lord came to Elijah the Tishbite: "Go down to meet Ahab king of Israel, who rules in Samaria. He is now in Naboth's vineyard, where he has gone to take possession of it. Say to him, 'This is what the Lord says: Have you not murdered a man and seized his property?' Then say to him, 'This is what the Lord says: In the place where dogs licked up Naboth's blood, dogs will lick up your blood—yes, yours!'"

Ahab said to Elijah, "So you have found me, my enemy!"

*"I have found you," he answered, "because you have sold
yourself to do evil in the eyes of the Lord. He says, 'I am going
to bring disaster on you. I will wipe out your descendants and
cut off from Ahab every last male in Israel—slave or free. I will
make your house like that of Jeroboam son of Nebat and that of
Baasha son of Ahijah, because you have aroused my anger and
have caused Israel to sin.'*

*"And also concerning Jezebel the Lord says: 'Dogs will devour
Jezebel by the wall of Jezreel.'*

*"Dogs will eat those belonging to Ahab who die in the city, and
the birds will feed on those who die in the country."*

*(There was never anyone like Ahab, who sold himself to do evil
in the eyes of the Lord, urged on by Jezebel his wife. He behaved
in the vilest manner by going after idols, like the Amorites the
Lord drove out before Israel.)*

*When Ahab heard these words, he tore his clothes, put on
sackcloth and fasted. He lay in sackcloth and went
around meekly.*

*Then the word of the Lord came to Elijah the Tishbite: "Have
you noticed how Ahab has humbled himself before me? Because
he has humbled himself, I will not bring this disaster in his day,
but I will bring it on his house in the days of his son."*

When Ahab got that word from the Lord he repented of
his sins.

The key word is repent. No matter how much sin you've done and God will forgive you.

1 Timothy 1:12-14:

I thank Christ Jesus our Lord, who has given me strength, that he considered me trustworthy, appointing me to his service. Even though I was once a blasphemer and a persecutor and a violent man, I was shown mercy because I acted in ignorance and unbelief. The grace of our Lord was poured out on me abundantly, along with the faith and love that are in Christ Jesus.

183 I AM A GOOD PERSON:

That's not enough to be a good person, you've got to repent of your sins, and receive Jesus as your Lord and Savior.

Isaiah 64:6:

All of us have become like one who is unclean, and all our righteous acts are like filthy rags; we all shrivel up like a leaf, and like the wind our sins sweep us away.

Luke 18:19:

"Why do you call me good?" Jesus answered. No one is good— except God alone.

Jesus, who is perfect did not call Himself good.

1 John 3:10:

...Anyone who does not do what is right is not God's child, nor is anyone who does not love their brother and sister.

184 I GO TO CHURCH:

That's not enough to go to church. A lot of people are in the church but they are not in God. Going to church is not going to save you. You go to church to learn how to live right, to fellowship, to worship, to be strengthened, encouraged, lifted up, to get spiritual insight, and growth. To hear the word which changes your life if you do what the word says.

2 Timothy 3:5:
They will go to church, yes, but they won't really believe anything they hear. Don't be taken in by people like that-(From the Book)

One day I was getting dressed for church and the Lord said, "People think going to church is serving God." Serving God is helping people.

John 12:26:
Whoever serves me must follow me...

1 Peter 1:16:
For it is written: "Be holy, because I am holy."[

185 I GOT BAPTIZED:

People don't know what it means to get baptized. To be baptized is an outward sign of an inward change in your heart. You should not get baptized if you're not sorry for your sins, and ready to change your life, not just stop drinking or smoking or going to clubs, but repent of your sins. Repent means to be sorry for the sins you've done and to turn from your ways to God's ways. Your mind, attitude and behavior is to change. If you don't change, don't get baptized because it will be in vain. It will not get you in heaven. When we go down in the water it's washing away our old way of life. When we come up it's to a new life in Christ Jesus. Baptism is as sacred as taking communion. Anybody can't baptize you. They have to be saved themselves, and living in God's will. People have misused baptism, not knowing why they should be baptized. They join a church and get baptized with no intention of turning their life around.

Luke 3:10-14:
The crowd replied, what do you want us to do?

"If you have two coats," he replied, "Give one to the poor. If you have extra food give it away to those who are hungry." Even tax collectors–notorious for their corruption–came to be baptized and asked, "How shall we prove to you that we have abandoned our sins?"

"By your honesty," he replied.

"Make sure you collect no more taxes than the Roman government required you to."

"And us," asked some soldiers. "What about us?"

John replied "Don't extort money by threats and violence, don't accuse anyone of what you know he didn't do, and be content with your pay." The Book

Galatians 3:27:
For all of you who were baptized into Christ have clothed yourselves with Christ.

Acts 22:16:

...Get up, be baptized and wash your sins away, calling on his name.

186 I THINK I AM:

This is something you'll know, I'll tell them you're not if you don't know for sure. Because your life changes, you don't live the way you used to live. You have a personal relationship with the Lord. You spend time with the Lord, getting up early in the morning spending time with Him before your family gets up. You tell Him how much you love Him. Thanking Him for who He is, for all He's done for you. Thanking Him for how great He is, worshipping and loving on Him, you'll feel his presence and He'll talk to you also.

John 8:31-32:

..."If you hold to my teaching, you are really my disciples. Then you will know the truth, and the truth will set you free."

John 16:13:

But when he, the Spirit of truth, comes, he will guide you into all the truth. He will not speak on his own; he will speak only what he hears, and he will tell you what is yet to come.

187 I'LL WAIT UNTIL I'M ON MY DEATH BED

That's gambling with your soul; you may not be able to repent. You could die suddenly, and I do believe the devil will not let you remember to repent just before you die. You could die in your sleep.

One day my boss and I were leaving Carey Hillards and I saw four people talking and the Spirit said ask them about being saved. I did and the older man, he may be the father said he was a backslider. I said the Lord wants you to come back to Him. He said, "I'll repent on my death bed." I told him you might die in your sleep. He pointed to his wife and said she won't let me die in my sleep. He doesn't realize God may have been giving him a warning one last time before he die to repent. Death could have been right around the corner. He took it for a joke that his wife would not let him die in his sleep. This is a trick from the devil. He got people thinking they can live like the devil in their sins, and wait till they're dying to repent. God does take death bed repentance but not with that attitude.

Deuteronomy 6:16:
Ye shall not tempt the Lord your God... KJV

Matthew 4:7:
Jesus answered him, "It is also written: 'Do not put the Lord your God to the test.'

We're to live right then we will die right.

188 I PRAY TO MOTHER EARTH. I FOUND MY GOD IN NATURE:

How do you pray to the earth? What do you say?

Matthew 6:9-14:
"This, then, is how you should pray:

"'Our Father in heaven, hallowed be your name, your kingdom come, your will be done, on earth as it is in heaven. Give us today our daily bread. And forgive us our debts, as we also have

forgiven our debtors. And lead us not into temptation, but deliver us from the evil one. 'For if you forgive other people when they sin against you, your heavenly Father will also forgive you.

Prayer is communicating with God, and He talks back to you. How can the earth talk to you or help you. In times of trouble we call upon God for help for guidance. When things are going well we keep talking to Him and praising Him. It's like we talk to our parents and children. All children depend and look to their parents. They can't take care of themselves. God is our heavenly Father and we're to depend and look to Him for everything, because when we live our life ourself we make a mess. Only God can fix our mess, but we've got to pray to Him and ask for forgiveness of our sins. That's why rich people are killing themselves. There's a void in their heart that only God can fill. They buy things, travel around the world, drink, do drugs to try and fill the void and it just get worse, so instead of giving their life to God they kill themselves. God created nature and the earth.

Psalm 146:5-6:
Blessed are those whose help is the God of Jacob, whose hope is in the Lord their God. He is the Maker of heaven and earth, the sea, and everything in them—he remains faithful forever.

I've been going downtown since 2008. Last year in 2011 I noticed when I would approach some ladies they would pull their purse to them and step back from me as if I was going to beg them for money. So I said to myself, "I'll dress up." Sometimes I would be in a scrub top and jacket or if I wasn't coming from work I'd just dress casual, then I realized it was the devil since he could not stop me with tiredness, or when my knee was hurting, or when my feet was hurting, but I kept going. Some people think I'm trying to get them to come to my church. They will say I go to church. That's not enough. It's not about going to church, it's about being saved from your ways and your sins.

I would not ask other nationalities about being saved, because I thought they would not understand who I was talking about. Then one day in January, 2012, I was downtown and I started asking them, because they need to know about Jesus and salvation also. I thank God for that revelation. One young chinese man said Jesus is a good man, but he didn't say if he was saved or not. So now I know to ask "everybody."

~~101~~ NO 262 REASONS WHY THE SAINTS NEED TO WITNESS!

CHAPTER 8

You're Witnessing Wrong

189 YOU'RE WITNESSING WRONG:

She said she was saved and I was offending people by asking them that. I told her God told me to ask them "if they ever thought about being saved." and when I changed the way God told me to say it I messed it up. She was arguing in front of two unsaved men. When she left I asked the men did I offend them and they said no. When God tells you to do something, He doesn't tell two or three people. He tells you, and it's up to you to obey God or man.

Acts 4:19:
But Peter and John replied, "Which is right in God's eyes: to listen to you, or to him?...

190 ONE LADY SAID THAT'S WRONG ASKING PEOPLE ABOUT BEING SAVED. YOU SHOULD ASK THEM IF THEY HAVE A JOB OR DO THEY WANT A CIGARETTE:

She was mad because the man I asked about being saved, had

asked her for a cigarette. I told her no, God told me to ask that,
I was concerned for their souls.

Genesis 12:1:
The Lord had said to Abram, "Go from your country, your
people and your father's household to the land I will show you.

I'm sure Abram's family tried to talk him out of going, but if
you know the voice of God, do what He tells you to do.

191 I'M SINNING. I'M BLASPHEMING BECAUSE I SAID JESUS IS THE SON OF GOD:

This man hollered this at me and kept on walking.

Matthew 10:32-33:
"Whoever acknowledges me before others, I will also
acknowledge before my Father in heaven. But whoever disowns
me before others, I will disown before my Father in heaven.

Mark 3:28-29:
Truly I tell you, people can be forgiven all their sins and every
slander they utter, but whoever blasphemes against the Holy
Spirit will never be forgiven; they are guilty of an eternal sin."

192 YOU'RE TRYING TO SAVE PEOPLE. YOU'RE GOING TO HELL YOURSELF!:

This man is a Muslim, but I've seen him in a couple of
Holiness Churches several years ago. He would never say
anything. He would just sit and listen then leave. When I saw

him years later he was in a wheel chair and he hollered this to me as I was witnessing.

Mark 1:17:
"Come, follow me," Jesus said, "and I will send you out to fish for people."

Acts 1:8:
But you will receive power when the Holy Spirit comes on you; and you will be my witnesses in Jerusalem, and in all Judea and Samaria, and to the ends of the earth.

193 I'M GOD:

This is the same man who said I was going to hell. I saw him about a year later. He was in a wheel chair. I asked him "if he ever thought about being saved," and he said, "I am God." He said he was fighting with the police and they shot him, and he's paralyzed and said if he wasn't God he would not be able to move his toes. I couldn't get through to him that he's wrong so I left. I realized when he was coming to those holiness churches he was hearing the truth, but he didn't accept it. He doesn't realize that God is a spirit, a Holy Spirit. Jesus was giving him a chance but he hardened his heart against the truth.

John 4:24:
God is spirit, and his worshipers must worship in the Spirit and in truth.

194 STOP FEEDING PEOPLE THAT GARBAGE!:

I had asked this man who said he was a muslim. About two days later he saw me asking people. As he walked by he said

"Stop feeding people that garbage," and kept walking. I said to myself if I see him again I'm going to anoint him in the name of Jesus but I never saw him again.

1 Corinthians 1:18:
For the message of the cross is foolishness to those who are perishing, but to us who are being saved it is the power of God.

195 INSTEAD OF BEING OUT HERE HARASSING PEOPLE YOU SHOULD BE HOME PROTECTING YOURSELF:

I told him God is protecting me as long as I'm doing his work.

Isaiah 51:12-15:
I even I am He who comforts you. Who are you that you should fear mortal men, the sons of men, who are but grass. That you forget the Lord your maker...that you live in constant fear.

If I stop witnessing and stay home I'd be living in terror, and not trusting God.

Matthew 5:11 & 12:
Blessed are you when people insult you, persecute you and falsely say all kinds of evil against you because of me. Rejoice and be glad, because great is your reward in heaven, for in the same way they persecuted the prophets who were before you.

John 15:20:
...If they persecuted me, they will persecute you also, if they obeyed my teaching, they will obey yours also. They will treat you this way because of my name, for they do not know the One who sent Me.

197 IT'S TOO LATE:

I was talking to 5 teenage boys, telling them when they get saved they can't continue in their sins, having sex. One of them said it's too late. I've already had sex. I told him to repent, ask God to forgive him. For those who are saved and having sex outside of marriage "stop" because judgment is upon the church, repent and get married or wait on your spouse. He was about 15!

Acts 4:2:
Peter replied, "Repent and be baptized, everyone of you, in the name of Jesus Christ for the forgiveness of your sins. And you will receive the gift of the Holy Spirit.

198 I'M TOO YOUNG:

I can't remember if this was a boy or girl, but God save children, teenager, adults, senior citizens, anyone who repents and accepts Jesus as their Lord and Savior.

Ecclesiastes 12:1:
Remember your creator in the days of your youth, before the trouble come and the year approach when you will say, I find no pleasure in them.

Jeremiah 1:6-8:
"Alas, Sovereign Lord," I said, "I do not know how to speak; I am too young."

But the Lord said to me, "Do not say, 'I am too young.' You must go to everyone I send you to and say whatever I command you. Do not be afraid of them, for I am with you and will rescue you," declares the Lord.

1 Timothy 4:12

Don't let anyone look down on you because you are young, but set and example for the believers in speech, in life, in love, in faith and in purity.

I know a preacher, James Farmer, who was preaching at the age of six. I met him when he was in his 40's. There is a 17 year old Evangelist who visits my church often, so you're never too young or old for God to use you.

199 I GOT HURT IN CHURCH:

This is the worst hurt because you trust and believe that the church people are of God, and they're the last ones you think would hurt you. The devil use this hurt to keep people out of church and away from God. Especially new saints, baby Christians. People don't realize when you get hurt, disappointed in church by the pastor, etc that's the main time to fast and pray. People don't fast anymore, we need to go back to the old landmark of fasting and praying. A lady said a deacon came to her house and she went to the bathroom. When she came out he was standing naked in her bedroom with only his socks on. And that scared her back out into the world. One man said the church mistreated his grandmother when she was sick and died. He doesn't want anything to do with church. I told them to pray and ask God to send them to a church, because every church is not of God, every pastor God did not send. This is a trick of the devil that is keeping a lot of people from coming back to God.

Matthew 18:7:
Woe to the world because of the things that cause people to sin!
Such things must come, but woe to the man through whom
they come!

Romans 14:12 &13:
So then each of us will give an account of himself to God.

Therefore let us stop passing judgment on one another, instead
make up your mind not to put any stumbling block or obstacle
in your brother's way.

About two months ago I was leaving work and saw two ladies talking on the porch. I didn't witness then. I got condemned so I turned around and asked them if they ever thought about being saved. One said she was. That she got hurt in church and wasn't going to any church. She said it was a small family church, and that she couldn't pay tithe because she did not have any income coming in. She said the pastor asked her what your financial income was. She told her she didn't have any, so she asked do my husband get income tax. I overlooked that. Then my aunt died and left me some custom jewelry. When I wore it to church they said if you can buy jewelry you can give money to the church. The whole church was making remarks about me not giving when I didn't have it to give. I felt like the church was full of mess. I left! Thank God for sending an Evangelist to witness to me. She got my number and I started going to church with her. If she had not come by I probably would have went back in the world. I told my son and his girlfriend they are going to church next Sunday.

I met a young lady at the bus stop and she said when she was about eight years old, she was at a church with her mother and they were throwing chairs. She said it scared her, She looked around and the whole church was on the floor. She and her mother never went back. Well, I witness to her and invited her to my church, so prayerfully she'll come and bring her mother.

200 I'VE GOT TO GET A JOB FIRST:

If that's the case the devil won't let you get a job.

Luke 12:31:
But seek his kingdom, and these things will be given to you as well.

201 I'M IN A SITUATION:

He said he couldn't get saved until he got his life right. You can't get your life right without God.

Matthew 11:28-30:
Come to me, all you who are weary and heavy burden, and I will give you rest. Take my yoke upon you and learn of me, for I am gentle and humble in heart, and you will find rest for your weary soul. For my yoke is easy and my burden is light.

John 10:10:
The thief comes only to steal and kill and destroy, I have come that they may have life, and have it to the full.

202 I PLEAD THE FIFTH:

This was a strange answer.

John 12:48:
There is a judge for the one who rejects me, and does not accept my words.

203 NOT TODAY, MAYBE TOMORROW:

Hebrew 14:7:
...today if you hear his voice harden not your hearts.

James 4:14:
Why, you do not even know what will happen tomorrow. What is your life? You are a mist that appears for a little while and then vanishes.

204 I'M GOING TO KEEP MY LIFE. I SAVED MYSELF:

He said this after I asked him if he ever thought about being saved, giving his life to Jesus.

Mark 8:35:
For whoever wants to save his life will lose it, but whoever loses his life for me and for the gospel will save it. What good is it for a man to gain the whole world, yet forfeit his soul? Or what can a man give in exchange for his soul?

205 I BELIEVE IN IDEALS

206 I'M FROM CANADA:

I said you can be saved in Canada, She said, Oh No!

207 I HAVE DIFFERENT THINGS GOING ON IN THAT DEPARTMENT.

208 THAT'S NONE OF YOUR BUSINESS.

209 MY BOSS IS ONE OF THEM.

210 NO, NO, NO. I WOULDN'T DO THAT:

For the answers to 202 - 210.

Romans 2:6-11:
God will give to each person according to what he has done. To those who by persistence in doing good seek glory, honor and immortality he will give eternal life. But for those who are self seeking and who reject the truth and follow evil, there will be wrath and anger. There will be trouble and distress for every human being who does evil: first for the Jew, then for the Gentile, but glory, honor and peace for everyone who does good; first for the Jew, then for the Gentile. For God does not show favoritism.

211 I'M TO OLD, I DON'T HAVE TIME:

That's a poor excuse; you're never too old to be saved. He looked to be in his 40's.

Joshua 14:16:
...Caleb said to Joshua...I was forty years old at the time Moses had sent us from Kadesh Barnea to spy out the land of Canaan.

I reported what I felt was truth...Now as you see, from that time until now the Lord has kept me alive and well for all these forty-five years, since crisscrossing the wilderness, and today I am eighty-five years old. I am as strong now as I was when Moses sent us on that journey, and I can still travel and fight as well as I could then. The Book

Joel 2:28:
...I will pour out my spirit on all people. Your sons and daughters will prophesy. Your old men will dream dreams, your young men will see visions.

212 ARE YOU TRYING TO SCARE ME?:

I was telling this man what Jesus said would be the signs that He's coming soon. We won't be able to tell summer from winter, there would be bloodshed in the streets. I said, "no, I'm just telling you that the signs of Jesus return is here now."

Matthew 24:3-4:
...What events will signal your return and the end of the world, Jesus told them. Don't let anyone fool you. For many will come claiming to be the Messiah, and will lead many astray. When you hear of wars beginning, this does not signal my return, these must come but the end is not yet. The nations and kingdoms of the earth will rise against each other and there will be famine and earthquakes in many place.s But all this will only be the beginning of the horrors to come. Then you will be tortured and killed and hated all over the world because you are mine, and many of you shall fall back into sin and betray and hate each other. And many false prophets will appear and lead many astray. Sin will be rampant everywhere and will cool the love of many. But those enduring to the end shall be saved. And the

Good News about the kingdom will be preached throughout the whole world, so that all nations will hear it, and then finally the end will come. The Book

1 John 2:18:
Dear children, this is the last hour and as you have heard that the antichrist is coming, even now many antichrist have come.

213 YOU SAID YOU WERE GOING TO ASK ME ONE QUESTION, YOU ASKED TWO:

I knew this lady for about 30 years. We used to work together and I never asked her about being saved. I saw her downtown one day and I said let me ask you one thing. So I asked her, and she said she had thought about and know all about it all her life. I asked if she was living it? She said, "You said you were going to ask me one. I gave you the answer now you're asking another. No, I'm not living it. God knows when He's ready for me."

I said, "He's ready now. You've lived all these years, what are you waiting for?"

She said, "God will let me know when it's time. I'm waiting on God." I said, "No God's waiting on you."

Then she said she had to go. She's in her late 60's. A lot of people had this excuse I'm waiting on God. He sends people to you to witness to you. He gives you the thought to be saved. You did nothing about being saved on your own. That's God giving you that mind. What else you want him to do? Sky write it? You would still make an excuse.

214 YOU DON'T HAVE TO BE SAVED TO GO TO HEAVEN.

215 YOU DON'T HAVE TO GO TO CHURCH TO GO TO HEAVEN:

If that was true Jesus died in vain.

John 3:3-5:
Jesus replied, "Very truly I tell you, no one can see the kingdom of God unless they are born again."

"How can someone be born when they are old?" Nicodemus asked. "Surely they cannot enter a second time into their mother's womb to be born!"

Jesus answered, "Very truly I tell you, no one can enter the kingdom of God unless they are born of water and the Spirit.

Hebrews 9:27-28:
Just as people are destined to die once, and after that to face judgment, so Christ was sacrificed once to take away the sins of many; and he will appear a second time, not to bear sin, but to bring salvation to those who are waiting for him.

Mark 1:21:
...Jesus went into the synagogue and began to teach.

Mark 3:1:
Another time Jesus went into the synagogue, and a man with a shriveled hand was there.

Hebrews 10:25:

...not giving up meeting together, as some are in the habit of doing...

So the Bible says we've got to be saved and go to church to stay saved.

216 WITNESSING WAS FOR THE 70'S:

This lady said her mother is a pastor and she knew all about salvation and didn't want to hear about salvation, that it was for the 70's.

Jesus told the disciples in Acts that they will be witnesses to the end of the earth. He knew they would not be alive to reach the end of the earth, but for the ones coming after them to witness until Jesus come.

Acts 1:8:

But you will receive power when the Holy Spirit comes on you; and you will be my witnesses in Jerusalem, and in all Judea and Samaria, and to the ends of the earth.

Acts 22:15:

You will be his witness to all people of what you have seen and heard.

217 IF HE'S SAVED, I'M SAVED:

I asked two men. One said he was saved and the other didn't say anything. So I asked, "Are you saved?" He said, "If he's saved then I'm saved." I said, "You can't go on his salvation, you've got to know God for yourself."

Hebrews 8:11-12:
No longer will they teach their neighbor, or say to one another, 'Know the Lord,' because they will all know me, from the least of them to the greatest. For I will forgive their wickedness and will remember their sins no more.

218 EVERYBODY HAS THE HOLY SPIRIT:

He thought since God breathed breath into man that they got the Holy Spirit. So they are already saved. I tried to explain to him the Holy Spirit came at Pentecost and only on those who are saved.

Acts 1:5:
For John baptized with water, but in a few days you will be baptized with the Holy Spirit.

Acts 1:8:
But you will receive power when the Holy Spirit comes on you...

Acts 2:1-4:
When the day of Pentecost came, they were all together in one place. Suddenly a sound like the blowing of a violent wind came from heaven and filled the whole house where they were sitting. They saw what seemed to be tongues of fire that separated and came to rest on each of them. All of them were filled with the Holy Spirit and began to speak in other tongues as the Spirit enabled them.

219 OH YOU'RE SO FUNNY:

One lady said this after I asked her.

220 OH YOU WANT TO HAVE THAT CONVERSATION. I CAN'T HAVE THAT CONVERSATION, BUT THANK YOU:

One lady said this to me.

2 Timothy 3:1-4:
But mark this: There will be terrible times in the last days.
People will be lovers of themselves, lovers of money, boastful,
proud, abusive, disobedient to their parents, ungrateful, unholy,
without love, unforgiving, slanderous, without self-control,
brutal, not lovers of the good, treacherous, rash, conceited,
lovers of pleasure rather than lovers of God.

The more I go out to witness, the more rejections I get. I was going to name this book "*101 Reasons Why the Saints Need to Witness*" but the number kept growing. If I didn't cut it off there it would be so much more. I have asked several ladies who said they were saved and one had on shorts, so short you could see the bottom of her butt. One had on a blouse cut so low you could almost see her nipple. I told some of them that too much of their breast was showing. I told them you can't tell a man about Jesus because he won't hear anything you say, he'll be distracted by your breast, and that's causing men to lust after you. So you're causing men to sin and you are sinning by causing them to sin.

It's a shame the world dresses more modest than the saved do. For one thing, they're not being taught how to dress. Another thing they're trying to get a husband and think showing everything will attract a decent man, which it won't. That's dressing loose. What shocked me more was I visited a

Holiness Church and a choir member in her 60's had on a very low cut blouse and no one said anything to her. I told one of the ladies her blouse was cut too low. Since then, whenever I see her, she has on a decent top. She was in her 50's, some of the younger ones didn't want to hear it.

1 Timothy 2:9-10:

I also want the women to dress modestly, with decency and propriety, adorning themselves, not with elaborate hairstyles or gold or pearls or expensive clothes, but with good deeds, appropriate for women who profess to worship God.

In my Study Bible it says the women were trying to gain respect by looking beautiful rather than by becoming Christlike in character. Some thought that they could win an unbelieving husband to Christ through their appearance.

1 Peter 3:1-6:

Wives, fit in with your husband's plans, for then if they refuse to listen, when you talk to them about the Lord, they will be won by your respectful, pure, behavior. Your godly lives will speak to them better than any words. Don't be concerned about the outward beauty that depends on jewelry, or beautiful clothes, or hair arrangement. Be beautiful inside, in your hearts, with the lasting charm of a gentle and quiet spirit which is so precious to God. That kind of beauty was seen in the saintly woman of old, who trusted God and fitted in with their husband's plans. The Book

If you dress showing all your body before you got saved, once you're saved, you should dress decently, because you're representing Jesus. Wearing those short skin tight dresses is not godly. And you are not being an example for the unsaved.

221 WHICH JESUS, BLACK JESUS OR WHITE JESUS?:

I tried to explain to him, there's only one Jesus, there's no Jesus for black and then a Jesus for whites, or one for Jews.

Colossians 3:11:
Here there is no Gentile or Jew, circumcised or uncircumcised, barbarian, Scythian, slave or free, but Christ is all, and is in all.

222 THAT'S A MATTER I SHOULD TALK TO MY FAMILY ABOUT:

I asked three teenage girls and one of them said this, and kept on walking.

Matthew 10:37:
Anyone who loves their father or mother more than me is not worthy of me; anyone who loves their son or daughter more than me is not worthy of me.

Salvation is personal. It's between you and God, not between you, God and your parents.

223 SATAN IS SO MUCH FUN:

I said that hell's burning is not fun. He said bless you for trying.

We were all born with a sinful nature. Sinning comes easy, it's fun at the beginning but in the end it leads to depression, heartache, suicide, etc.

Galatians 5:19-21:

The acts of the sinful nature are obvious: sexual immorality, impurity, wild living, idolatry and witchcraft, hatred, discord, jealousy, fits of rage, selfish ambition, arguing, constant effort to get the best for yourself, complaints, and criticisms, the feeling that everyone is wrong except those in our group, wrong teaching, envy, murder, drunkenness, wild parties, and all sorts of things. Let me tell you again as I have before, that anyone living that sort of life will not inherit the kingdom of God. The Book

Romans 13:13:

Don't spend your time in wild parties and getting drunk or in adultery and lust, or fighting or jealousy. But ask the Lord Jesus Christ to help you live as you should,and don't make plans to enjoy evil. The Book

Hebrews 11:24-25:

By faith Moses, when he had grown up, refused to be known as the son of Pharaoh's daughter. He chose to be mistreated along with the people of God rather than to enjoy the fleeting pleasures of sin.

224 THIS MAN HELD HIS HANDS UP, SAID NO THAT'S NOT IN MY CONVERSATION. SORRY.

225 THIS MAN SAID YOU DON'T WANT TO KNOW MY ANSWER ON THAT ONE THERE:

We are blessed to believe and accept Jesus as our Lord and Savior.

226 I DON'T BELIEVE HE WAS A MIRACLE WORKER, JUST A FAST TALKER:

I said. "Oh no, He is the Son of God."

He said, "How do you know that?"

I said, "I believe the Bible."

John 17:8:
For I gave them the words you gave me and they accepted them. They knew with certainty that I came from you, and they believed that you sent me.

John 17:20-21:
My prayer is not for them alone. I pray also for those who will believe in me through their message, that all of them may be one, Father, just as you are in me and I am in you. May they also be in us so that the world may believe that you have sent me.

John 20:29:
Then Jesus told him, "Because you have seen me, you have believed; blessed are those who have not seen and yet have believed."

Jesus did many other miraculous signs in the presence of His disciples, which are not recorded in this book. But these are written that you may believe that Jesus is the Christ, the Son of God, and that believing you may have life in his name.

I thank God all the time for believing in Jesus, in the Bible for believing in God, but it's not enough to believe. We've got to obey the Bible and do what it says.

227 YOU'RE SELFISH FOR WITNESSING:

It was four ladies and one of them said, it was stupid to ask people about being saved. She said she was saved. I said, "God told me to ask." She started hollering, "No, he didn't; you're just being selfish. You think by doing this God will like you more."

I tried to talk to her but she got louder and louder saying, "You're selfish; you think God's going to like you more."

People across the street were looking at us because she was so loud. I walked away, she went across the street still hollering, "You're selfish. You just want God to like you more."

She was highly upset. I was in shock to hear that, to think she is supposed to be saved and would say such a thing. But I also realize everybody who say they are saved are not. A lot of people think joining the church and getting baptized that they are a Christian or they are saved.

1 Timothy 5:21:
I charge you, in the sight of God and Christ Jesus and the elect angels, to keep these instructions without partiality, and to do nothing out of favoritism.

James 2:1:

My brothers and sisters, believers in our glorious Lord Jesus Christ must not show favoritism.

1 Peter 1:17:

Since you call on a Father who judges each person's work impartially, live out your time as foreigners here in reverent fear.

228 I CAN'T BE UNSAVED:

I said, "Yes you can if you continue to sin."

Then she said, "I like all the sex, drugs and alcohol. I'm cool with Jesus and He's cool with me. Thank You," and then turned away. She didn't want to hear anything I said.

1 Thessalonians 4:3-8:

It is God's will that you should be sanctified: that you should avoid sexual immorality; that each of you should learn to control your own body in a way that is holy and honorable, not in passionate lust like the pagans, who do not know God...The Lord will punish all those who commit such sins...For God did not call us to be impure, but to live a holy life.

Romans 6:12:

Therefore do not let sin reign in your mortal body so that you obey its evil desires. Do not offer any part of yourself to sin as an instrument of wickedness, but rather offer yourselves to God...For sin shall no longer be your master, because you are not under the law, but under grace.

1 John 3:9-10:

No one who is born of God will continue to sin, because God's seed remains in them; they cannot go on sinning, because they have been born of God. This is how we know who the children of God are and who the children of the devil are: Anyone who does not do what is right is not God's child, nor is anyone who does not love their brother and sister.

229 YOU NEED TO MAKE AN APPOINTMENT:

This man said this. He didn't want to talk about it.

Hebrews 3:15:
..."Today, if you hear his voice, do not harden your hearts...

230 I'M LIVING BY WHAT SEEMS GOD FOR ME.

231 I HAVE MY VERSION OF WHAT'S RIGHT FOR ME. I DON'T AGREE WITH THE BIBLE:

I was telling her the things the Bible said we are to do and not to do.

Proverbs 14:12:
There is a way that appears to be right, but in the end it leads to death.

232 I HEARD HE WAS COMING FOR YEARS:

I told him God is giving people a chance to repent. People don't realize if Jesus comes back today or tomorrow a lot of people will go to hell, even those that are saved and still sinning.

2 Peter 3:3-4 & 8-9:
Above all, you must understand that in the last days scoffers will come, scoffing and following their own evil desires. They will say, "Where is this 'coming' he promised? Ever since our ancestors died, everything goes on as it has since the beginning of creation."

But do not forget this one thing, dear friends: With the Lord a day is like a thousand years, and a thousand years are like a day. The Lord is not slow in keeping his promise, as some understand slowness. Instead he is patient with you, not wanting anyone to perish, but everyone to come to repentance.

He looked like he was about to cry as I was talking to him. He said I had witnessed to him before. I asked, "Did you ask God to help you to give up your ways to repent and ask God to save you?" I hope this time he's taken it to heart and repented.

2 Peter 3:10-11:
But the day of the Lord will come like a thief. The heavens will disappear with a roar; the elements will be destroyed by fire, and the earth and everything done in it will be laid bare. Since everything will be destroyed in this way, what kind of people ought you to be? You ought to live holy and godly lives

233 ONE MAN SAID, "NOT EVEN CLOSE."

234 NO, I'M GAY. HE DON'T LIKE ME:

I said, "Jesus loves you."

The gays think that Jesus doesn't love them because of their lifestyle but he still loves them. He doesn't like the life they're living. Sin is sin. He'll forgive you just like he would a thief or murderer.

235 GOD DON'T WANT ME:

I said, "Yes he does. He loves you."

1 John 4:9:
This is how God showed his love among us: He sent his one and only Son into the world that we might live through him.

John 3:16:
For God so loved the world that he gave his one and only Son, that whoever believes in him shall not perish but have eternal life.

236 IT'S ON MY TO DO LIST.

237 I DON'T WANT TO BE SAVED.

238 OH NO, I'M GOOD. I REALLY DON'T WANT TO BE SAVED.

239 OH GOD NO, WE'RE JEWISH:

It's so sad people don't realize their soul is at stake. And there will be no excuse when they stand before God on judgment day. Because it will be revealed to them when someone witnessed to them or tried to and they rejected them.

240 THAT'S A DUMB QUESTION:

I said, "You take that up with God. He told me to ask that." Then she said, "No you take that up with Jesus."

241 THEY PREACH AGAINST WOMEN PREACHERS:

I used to be saved. They don't have all the books in the Bible. I said, God told them what books to be in the Bible. He knew we don't need the ones that were left out. Then he said, I was saved. They preach against women preachers. I said get in a church that believe in women preachers. He kept making up excuses. Then he said, he's trying to get his two sons to go to church but they won't go. They look to be 10 and 11. I said, you're not being a good example, you don't go so they're following what you do.

2 Timothy 3:16-17:
All Scripture is God-breathed and is useful for teaching, rebuking, correcting and training in righteousness, so that the servant of God may be thoroughly equipped for every good work.

242 I'M ON THE OTHER TEAM:

"You know that team is going down to hell."

He said, "I know."

Revelation 20:10-15

And the devil, who deceived them, was thrown into the lake of burning sulfur, where the beast and the false prophet had been thrown. They will be tormented day and night for ever and ever.

Then I saw a great white throne and him who was seated on it. The earth and the heavens fled from his presence, and there was no place for them. And I saw the dead, great and small, standing before the throne, and books were opened. Another book was opened, which is the book of life. The dead were judged according to what they had done as recorded in the books. The sea gave up the dead that were in it, and death and Hades gave up the dead that were in them, and each person was judged according to what they had done. Then death and Hades were thrown into the lake of fire. The lake of fire is the second death. Anyone whose name was not found written in the book of life was thrown into the lake of fire.

So why serve the devil who will be thrown into the lake of fire? It's crazy to know you're on the losing side and stay there. Those who don't believe in Jesus, who don't accept Him as their Lord and Savior will end up in the lake of fire. It says in the 10th verse, the devil ***deceived*** them. The first death is a physical death; the second death is spiritual. With the first death your body dies. With the second death your soul is burning forever. We're not like animals that die and they're gone. We have a body, a soul and a spirit. Our body is just a covering for our soul, just like clothes is a covering for our body. When our clothes wear out or get too small or big, we get rid of them. We don't get rid of our body also. So when our body dies our soul either goes to God or to hell.

243 JESUS DIED FOR MY SINS. I DON'T HAVE TO GIVE THEM UP:

Several people think that Jesus died for our sins so it's okay to continue to sin and they will go to heaven. That they don't need to stop sinning or get their life right with God. I tell them yes, he died for our sins but He doesn't want us to keep on sinning. In the old testament, the people would go to the priest every year and he would offer up sacrifices and ask for forgiveness of their sins. They could not pray to God themselves. God wanted a relationship with each individual. That's why Jesus died for our sins, so we can confess and repent of our own sins and know God for ourselves. God hates sin and its says in **Romans 6:1: ...**"*Shall we go on sinning so that grace may increase?" God forbid.*

Jesus did not die for our sins for us to keep on sinning. He became the sacrifice; He gave His life for us and we're to give up our sinful life for Him. And to do this we have to be saved and have the Holy Spirit, and read and do what the Bible says.

Matthew 5:8:
Blessed are the pure in heart, for they will see God.

Your heart is not pure if you're sinning.

Matthew 5:43-45:

You have heard that it was said, 'Love your neighbor and hate your enemy.' But I tell you, love your enemies and pray for those who persecute you, that you may be children of your Father in heaven...

Matthew 6:14-15:

For if you forgive other people when they sin against you, your heavenly Father will also forgive you. But if you do not forgive others their sins, your Father will not forgive your sins.

Nobody can love their enemy and pray for good things to happen to them unless they're saved. And if we don't do what the Bible tells us to do we're not obeying God.

1 Corinthians 6:9-11:

Or do you not know that wrongdoers will not inherit the kingdom of God? Do not be deceived: Neither the sexually immoral nor idolaters nor adulterers nor men who have sex with men nor thieves nor the greedy nor drunkards nor slanderers nor swindlers will inherit the kingdom of God. And that is what some of you were. But you were washed, you were sanctified, you were justified in the name of the Lord Jesus Christ and by the Spirit of our God.

Romans 8:5-8:

Those who live according to the flesh have their minds set on what the flesh desires; but those who live in accordance with the Spirit have their minds set on what the Spirit desires. The mind governed by the flesh is death, but the mind governed by the Spirit is life and peace. The mind governed by the flesh is hostile to God; it does not submit to God's law, nor can it do so. Those who are in the realm of the flesh cannot please God.

Since Jesus died for our sins, some people think they can keep on sinning and go to heaven by just believing in Jesus. If that was the case, God would not have had men to write the Bible. The demon believes in Jesus. They're not going to heaven!

244 I DON'T WANT TO BE FORGIVEN. I DON'T FEEL GUILTY:

He said this and kept on walking.

Romans 3:19:
Now we know that whatever the law says, it says to those who are under the law, so that every mouth may be silenced and the whole world held accountable to God.

James 2:10:
For whoever keeps the whole law and yet stumbles at just one point is guilty of breaking all of it.

245 NOPE, I'M GOING TO HELL:

People don't realize the torture they will suffer for eternity.

Mark 9:43:
...It is better for you to enter life maimed than with two hands to go into hell, where the fire never goes out.

Luke 16:22-23 & 27-28:
...The rich man also died...In Hades, where he was in torment..."He answered, 'Then I beg you, father, send Lazarus to my family, for I have five brothers. Let him warn them, so that they will not also come to this place of torment.'

246 AS LONG AS I RESPECT PEOPLE AND MYSELF AND TRY TO DO RIGHT I'M SAVED:

Acts 16:29-31:

The jailer...asked, "Sirs, what must I do to be saved?" They replied, "Believe in the Lord Jesus, and you will be saved—you and your household."

Romans 10:9:

If you declare with your mouth, "Jesus is Lord," and believe in your heart that God raised him from the dead, you will be saved.

247 WHO PAID YOU FOR SAVING PEOPLE? YOU GET PAID DAILY OR WEEKLY?

His bus came and he said, "I'm saved now." He took it lightly, but salvation is no joke.

THE WRATH OF GOD:

Deuteronomy 7:10:

But those who hate him he will repay to their face by destruction; he will not be slow to repay to their face those who hate him.

Psalm 11: 5-6:

...the wicked, those who love violence, he hates with a passion. On the wicked he will rain fiery coals and burning sulfur; a scorching wind will be their lot.

Proverbs 12:22:

The Lord detests lying lips, but he delights in people who are trustworthy.

Proverbs 14:31:
Whoever oppresses the poor shows contempt for their Maker, but whoever is kind to the needy honors God.

Isaiah 5:18-24:
Woe to those who drag their sins behind them like a bullock on a rope. They even mock the Holy One of Israel and dare the Lord to punish them. Hurry up and punish us, O Lord, they say. We want to see what you can do. They say that what is right is wrong, and what is wrong is right, that black is white and white is black, bitter is sweet and sweet is bitter. Woe to those who are wise and shrewd in their own eyes! Woe to those who are heroes when it comes to drinking, and boasting about the liquor they can hold. They take bribes to pervert justice, letting the wicked go free and putting innocent men in jail. Therefore God will deal with them and burn them. They will disappear like straw on fire...The Book

Psalm 37:38
But all sinners will be destroyed; there will be no future for the wicked.

Hebrews 10:26-27:
If we deliberately keep on sinning after we have received the knowledge of the truth, no sacrifice for sins is left, but only a fearful expectation of judgment and of raging fire that will consume the enemies of God.

CHAPTER 9

My Family

248 COUSIN #1:

"I'm saved."

I was too stunned to say anything, because she's having an affair with a married man. She drinks, smokes dope and lives like the devil. I called her about a week later and told her she's not saved living like she is. And she said, "If I wasn't saved why people keep coming to me for advice?" I can't remember what I told her but just because people come to you for advice doesn't mean you're saved.

249 COUSIN #2:

"I've been all around the world."

What does this have to do with being saved? She was still in her sins. She didn't make sense out of what she was saying.

250 COUSIN #3:

"I'm all right; if I wasn't I wouldn't have my own house and a new car."

I've talked with other cousins. Some received the witness, some didn't but they're still in their sins.

1 Corinthians 6:9-10:

Or do you not know that wrongdoers will not inherit the kingdom of God? Do not be deceived: Neither the sexually immoral nor idolaters nor adulterers nor men who have sex with men nor thieves nor the greedy nor drunkards nor slanderers nor swindlers will inherit the kingdom of God.

251 BRENDA MUST BE CRAZY:

One aunt said she is a Baptist and she's alright. I told her she needs to be saved, and she needs the Holy Spirit. She talked so nice to me on the phone. Then she called my mother and asked her if I was drunk or crazy.

John 10:20:

...*"He is demon-possessed and raving mad. Why listen to him?"*

If they call Jesus crazy, don't be surprised when they call you crazy also. My mother and I laughed at my aunt. I know she doesn't know any better, but I hope she gets saved before she dies.

252 WHAT ABOUT ROBERT?:

I asked another aunt and she asked me what about Robert. He's my husband. I told her he know about Holiness. What she meant was that I'm talking to her about being saved and my husband is not saved. I'm to ask other people whether my family is saved or not.

253 WHAT ABOUT YOUR SON?:

I asked a young man that knows my son and he asked me, what about your son? I told him I did my part which is to tell and teach him. I thank God for the change in both their lives.

Acts 16:31:
..."Believe in the Lord Jesus, and you will be saved—you and your household."

1Corinthians 7:12-14:
To the rest I say this (I, not the Lord): If any brother has a wife who is not a believer and she is willing to live with him, he must not divorce her. And if a woman has a husband who is not a believer and he is willing to live with her, she must not divorce him. For the unbelieving husband has been sanctified through his wife, and the unbelieving wife has been sanctified through her believing husband. Otherwise your children would be unclean, but as it is, they are holy.

254 MY BROTHER:

I asked my brother. He said he was saved; I said saved from what because he was still sinning. He couldn't answer. He used to read the Bible daily, teach Bible study but there was no change in his life. You've got to do what you read, teach and preach.

James 1:22:

Do not merely listen to the word, and so deceive yourselves. Do what it says.

1 John 1:6:

If we claim to have fellowship with him and yet walk in the darkness, we lie and do not live out the truth.

255 A COUSIN:

I asked one of my male cousins, and he said he is saved. I asked, do you have the Holy Spirit. He hesitated. I said no you're not saved, he's living with his girlfriend. He's been a member of a church for years; but that's not salvation.

1 Corinthians 6:18:

Flee from sexual immorality. All other sins a person commits are outside the body, but whoever sins sexually, sins against their own body.

1 Corinthians 7:2:

But since sexual immorality is occurring, each man should have sexual relations with his own wife, and each woman with her own husband.

256 YOUNGER DAUGHTER:

She said, I'm Agnostic; I don't believe in any one religion. I've studied different religions and they all say some things that's good and some that's bad. It doesn't make sense to me. I don't know if there's a higher power or not. I don't believe in the killing God told people to do in the Bible, especially killing the kids. I don't believe in the Bible, because I believe it was misinterpreted. I think Jesus was made up by people to have something to believe in.I don't want a God to bless me with a promotion or car or house, when there are kids being molested. Why would a God let kids get molested? They're innocent; they need the blessing. I read this book about a man who was a missionary. After a while he was not happy doing mission work or his religion. So he left and studied different religions and came to the conclusion that there's no God. And that's a good book. And I agree with Oprah, she don't believe in God. She started a new religion. I don't look at the bad things as from the devil, or the good things from God. Things that happen are just life. This was about two years ago when I talked with her. When I talked with her last week she said, she prays but have an open mind to other religions. When I first talked with her I was shocked. I said to myself, she is antichrist–the devil is a liar. She was in a holiness church as a child and every word of truth will rise up in her unto salvation.

257 MY SON:

Two weeks ago we were in church and the minister was walking down the aisle and stopped in front of him and made a gesture with his hands almost in his face. Well, he stayed through the service, but when we came up for prayer he walked out the church. I called him but he kept going. I thought he was going to start walking home. I was surprised to see him leaning on the car when we got out. So I thought he was going to argue, but he didn't. He said, "I'll call you when you get home."

To my surprise again he was calm and told me why he left. I told him the minister didn't realize what he did, that it was the devil wanting you to get upset. I've been telling him for a year to think positive and talk positive. That's what the message was that night, thinking and talking positive. He said he needed to hear that.

I thank God for his healing. He used to take medication. It had him sleeping all the time so he stopped taking it. I started praying with him almost every day binding the spirit of Bipolar and binding his mind to the mind of Jesus. Thank God I see the change.

258 MY OLDEST DAUGHTER:

She goes to the House of Prayer. She was in my church about six years ago. As a child the Lord would give her dreams and days later they would come to pass. Now she doesn't believe in women preachers, or the gift God gave her. My pastor is a woman and I'm an Evangelist. Just like I said before the devil is a liar. I took my kids to church when they were young, but that's not enough. You've got to teach them about God yourself. Most of them are not listening, most of the adults are not listening.

One day as we were walking home from a church I visited when they were small, the Lord showed me my heart was a brick wall and the word was bouncing off my heart like a ball bouncing off a wall. He was showing me, I was not taking in what I heard. So it's important to teach our kids so they can get a good understanding of God from their parents, if the parent's heart is right.

Proverbs 22:6:
Start children off on the way they should go, and even when they are old they will not turn from it.

2 Timothy 1:5:
I am reminded of your sincere faith, which first lived in your grandmother Lois and in your mother Eunice and, I am persuaded, now lives in you also.

Timothy's grandmother and mother taught him about Jesus at home. They didn't wait until they went to church.

Joel 2:28 and Acts 2:17:
And afterward, I will pour out my Spirit on all people. Your sons and daughters will prophesy...

Acts 16:30-31:
..."Sirs, what must I do to be saved? They replied, "Believe in the Lord Jesus, and you will be saved—you and your household."

259 MY MOTHER:

I've never thought about it.

I said, "You know, you've got to be saved to go to heaven."

She said, "Yeah,"

I said, "Ask God to help you to give up because these are the last days."

She said, "Yes, you're right." I've witnessed to her a couple of times before, but she need to be reminded.

261 MY HUSBAND:

He said, "Being saved is being honest under any circumstance. Once you lie, you step out of the boundaries of that relationship. If you're going to be Godly it's best to be honest. I know God has a job for me to do. Jesus came to me in a dream and told me He was going to bless me. The only time you should hurt someone is in defense of yourself or your family. I don't like calling out who gave what in church, because the person who gave $100.00 can afford it. The one who gave $1.00 probably gave all they had. You've got to be one way in life down with God or down with the devil."

The devil will really cry when Robert gets saved because now he's doing things that saved people are supposed to be doing. One time he went to visit one of his friends in jail, and a lady was there visiting her boyfriend or husband and she had on a blouse that was too revealing and they wouldn't let her see him, so Robert took off his shirt and gave it to her. He came home without his shirt. He's always giving money to people or taking them places.

Sometimes I get upset with all he does. He does more than the saved people. One day I was praying for him and the Spirit let me know to change his name. Don't say 'Robert', so when I pray for him I say Paul. I'm believing for the mantle of Paul to be on him. Then about two or three days later I was on our prayer line when the minister's husband who started the prayer line Evangelist Tucker told me to stop calling him Robert. Call him one of the men names in the Bible. I chose Paul because I'm claiming him to be like Paul.

I tell the devil all the time that Robert and I will be preaching the word of God together. Not only Robert but my whole family.

Praise God!

MY THOUGHT:

I didn't know anything about being saved until I was 16 years old. Before that I thought God weighed your good and bad on a scale. If your bad outweighed your good you went to hell. I just knew for sure I was going to heaven because I did not curse, fight, or get drunk. I'd drink when I went out to clubs. I didn't know until I got saved that I was evil, mean, stingy, and thought I was better than those who cursed and drink all the time. I was arrogant, full of pride which is all a sin. I thought I was a good person. Then I met my mother-in-law, Evangelist Orian Rhett, who taught me holiness. I didn't surrender right away. I still rebelled for years. I did get saved, but I did not give up my ways and sins. I was still jealous and thinking evil. She would call me up and tell me I wasn't right. Then I'd get a bad attitude toward her which was a sin. One day I told the Lord I don't want to be saved, just give me some money, a house to live in, a good life on earth and I'll go to hell. Another night I said, "Lord why you keep helping me when I keep messing up?" That night I had a dream that I was walking the street and there was people laying in the street. I would go to one and help them and walk a little distance and there was another laying in the street. I would help that one, and walk a little and see another and help that one. I can't remember what year that was . I know it was in the 80's. I didn't know what the dream meant until I started going out witnessing about 17 years later. I go downtown to the park. When I see them at the bus stop, I turn around in my car park and witness. Then I realized God was letting me know He kept helping me because one day I'll be helping others. Now I thank God so much for hearing and believing the truth, for living the truth. For Jesus is the way, the truth, and the life. *John 14:6*–having Jesus brings about a changed life. You think different. *John 10:10–...I have come that they may have life, and have it to the full.*

I would not have gotten into heaven with my way of thinking. I needed my sins to be forgiven not weighted. I've got the right attitude. I'm praying everyday to die daily to flesh, that I live in the spirit and not in flesh

I found out when you get an opportunity to witness to somebody do it then, because you might not get that opportunity again. It happened to me years ago. I was witnessing to a teenage girl and as I was leaving I heard the Spirit say, "Tell her more". I didn't, I said to myself I'll see her again and talk to her since we live in the same area, but I never saw her again. I repented for not obeying the Spirit.

MY SPOTS:

I was on a prayer line in Atlanta WWPP with Apostle J.B. Woods. She was talking about the sins in the saints' life. And I was agreeing with her, but saying it's not me. There's no sin in my life. Then one night I had a dream that I had on a white dress with spots on it the size of a quarter. I was shocked. I said not me, I don't have any spots. Well, the Lord told me that I had something in my heart against three people who were saved. He said call them, tell them what I have in my heart against them and ask them to forgive me and to pray for me, so I did. Then I saw myself as a garbage can and I was digging in myself pulling the garbage out.

Romans 12:3:-says *...Do not think of yourself more highly than you ought...* I was not backbiting, smoking, drinking, I paid my tithe, gave to everyone in need, but I had resentment in my heart which I covered up. I thought I was right with no sin in my life but **2 Corinthians 13:5** says *Examine yourselves to see whether you are in the faith; test yourselves....* We have to ask God to show us ourselves often, to search our heart and show us if anything is in our heart that He's not pleased with. If you are serious God will show you yourself.

I had a prayer partner who lives in Atlanta, and when we were praying God would bring names of people in other states for her to pray for that we didn't know. And she saw things. I didn't know she backslid because she kept on praying. Sometimes, I couldn't get in touch with her for days. She was lying and stealing, still praying, but the anointing was still in her life. She went back on drugs with the gifts still working in her. When I found out she was using me, we got into an argument and she said God has not done anything to me. It says in **Romans 11:29** *For God's gifts and his call are irrevocable.* That means God doesn't take the gifts and calling back when you sin. And the devil fools people, even Pastors, Evangelists, Prophets. If they sin they are still healing, still prophecying etc. They think God is letting them get away but it says in **Romans 2:9 & 11** *There will be trouble and distress for every human being who does evil...For God does not show favoritism.*

If you sin and don't stop you will go to hell. There's a lot of gifts in hell. She reaped what she sowed. She's a caregiver and she was taking care of a man who left his house to her, but the lady she was working for took the house from her and she didn't find out that she was left the house until two years later. She stole from me. The lady stole from her.

Job 4:8:
As I have observed, those who plow evil and those who sow trouble reap it.

Proverbs 22:8:
Whoever sows injustice reaps calamity, and the rod they wield in fury will be broken.

Galatians 6:7-8:
Do not be deceived: God cannot be mocked. A man reaps what he sows. Whoever sows to please their flesh, from the flesh will reap destruction; whoever sows to please the Spirit, from the Spirit will reap eternal life.

Romans 12:1:
Therefore, I urge you, brothers and sisters, in view of God's mercy, to offer your bodies as a living sacrifice, holy and pleasing to God—this is your true and proper worship.

Just like we presented our body to sin, when you're saved give your life to God completely. If you're not married and having sex you're not offering your body as a living sacrifice. Stop sinning, wait on the Lord. Ask Him for a spouse. If you asked and it's been years and He has not given you a spouse, check yourself. Maybe there's something in your life that's not pleasing to God. I was an unwed mother with three kids in my 30's. The younger women in my church were getting married. So I asked God to send me a husband. I waited a while. There was another wedding at the church. So I changed the way I asked. I said Lord, "Send me a husband to help me raise these kids while they're young." And he told me "I want you to live and let women know they can live without a man."

I was living in the project where women were changing men the way they change clothes. Then I visited a church and the message was "Wait on the Lord!!" Well I waited three months and married my husband who was not saved. I was disobedient to the Bible and there was so much trouble mainly on my side, which caused so much heartache for us. I was presenting my body a living sacrifice until I met him, then I started fornicating which is a sin. We did get married, but it was not time. God wanted and needed to do a work in my life and wanted Robert saved.

1 Corinthians 6:13:
...The body, however, is not meant for sexual immorality but for the Lord, and the Lord for the body.

1 Corinthians 6:18:
Flee from sexual immorality. All other sins a person commits are outside the body, but whoever sins sexually, sins against their own body.

Do you not know that your body is a temple of the Holy Spirit, who is in you, whom you have received from God? You are not your own. You were bought at a price. Therefore honor God with your body.

2 Corinthians 6:14:

Do not be yoked together with unbelievers. For what do righteousness and wickedness have in common? Or what fellowship can light have with darkness.

What harmony is there between Christ and Belial? What does a believer have in common with an unbeliever?

Romans 12:2:

Do not conform to the pattern of this world, but be transformed by the renewing of your mind. Then you will be able to test and approve what God's will is—his good, pleasing and perfect will.

A Christian should not let their children dress up or go to halloween parties or go trick or treating. That's of the devil. We are not to get tattoos.

Leviticus 19:28:

Do not cut your bodies for the dead or put tattoo marks on yourselves. I am the Lord.

One of the ministers in a church I was in wanted to get a tattoo of the cross on her, that's still a sin, even if it's a tattoo of Jesus.

I asked a couple about being saved. The lady pulled her bottom lip down and showed me a tattoo on the inside of her lip and walked off. I don't know what the tattoo was, I was shocked to see a tattoo in her mouth. Then another young lady had two horns sticking out her nose. I've seen several young people with them. We do not dress or follow the things the unsaved do. Jesus is our example. Would Jesus go get a tattoo? Would He cut His hair in a mohawk? Would He dress up in costumes? We're representing Jesus, so let the world see a difference in us. Be like Jesus. We're not to wear pajamas or night gown out in public. I have seen several people wearing their pajamas in stores in Pizza Hut. I even saw a lady downtown in her night gown. She went to pay her light bill in her night gown. This ought not be. Do you read your Bible at home, and if you do, you are supposed to do what it says. *Ephesians 5:1-2* says *Follow God's example...and walk in the way of love...* That there must not be even a hint of sexual immorality, or any kind of impurity or greed, among you, because that is improper for God's holy people.

We had a visiting preacher speaking at my church, Casetta Passmore-Heard and she was preaching on *Romans 12:1 &2*. One thing she said about the saints is so true and damaging to Holiness, is how the saints act so mean and nasty after church when they go out to eat especially on Sunday. She hears the waitresses talking about how nasty the saints act when their order is wrong. They're putting a bad reflection on Holiness, and they're keeping the unsaved from coming to Jesus. They see how ugly you're acting they will not come to church. Where is the change, if you acted like that before you got saved and you're still mean and impatient. You're walking in the flesh, and not in love. *1 Corinthians 13:4-5–Love is patient, love is kind. It does not envy, it does not boast, it is not proud. It does not dishonor others, it is not self-seeking...*

You're not walking in the fruit of the Spirit, you're still walking in your sinful nature. You're not showing Jesus. Would Jesus act the way you act? Is He mean and hateful? Is He rude? Put on the Fruit of the Spirit.

Galatians 5:22-24
But the fruit of the Spirit is love, joy, peace, forbearance, kindness, goodness, faithfulness, gentleness and self-control. Against such things there is no law. Those who belong to Christ Jesus have crucified the flesh with its passions and desires.

If you're acting ugly like that you're sinning, and you're keeping others from becoming saved. You're acting just like the Pharisees in **Matthew 23:13-14:** *Woe to you, teachers of the law and Pharisees, you hypocrites! You shut the door of the kingdom of heaven in people's faces. You yourselves do not enter, nor will you let those enter who are trying to.*

So change your ways and let's show Jesus; the only way the world will see Jesus is in our life.

2 Corinthians 5:17:
Therefore, if anyone is in Christ, the new creation has come...

This means our old mean nasty ways are gone, and our new nature in Christ to act like Jesus will act. Here's a secret saints: "Hell will be hotter for those sliding in from a church pew."

And there is a special section in hell for Pastors, Evangelists, Prophets and all who are leaders, but are sinning. You will be tormented much, much more than those who are not saved. Read the book *"Devine Revelation of Hell."*

And some of you are the worst tippers. You make Jesus ashamed to be called your Savior.

Hebrews 10:26-27:
If we deliberately keep on sinning after we have received the knowledge of the truth, no sacrifice for sins is left, but only a fearful expectation of judgment and of raging fire that will consume the enemies of God.

CHAPTER 10

Comments From Saved People

- One lady got mad because I didn't see Jesus in her. She said, "I'm saved you can't tell?" She said it in such a nasty way. When I asked the "saved" they look at me in such a strange way.

- One lady said she was saved and I shouldn't ask people that way. I said, "God told me what to say and I'm doing it like He told me to do it."

She said, "You're doing it wrong."

I said, "You tell God about it, because I changed what I ask people and I messed up."

We were downtown and she was arguing in front of two unsaved men that I had asked if they ever thought about being saved. She said I had asked her this several years ago and she asked the Lord to run into me again to correct me. She said she does it a different way. I didn't like the fact that she was arguing in front of the unsaved. When she got on the bus I asked the two men if I offended them by the way I asked them, and they said no. A lot of the saved answer me so mean. I get a few saved people who say, "I am saved, thank you for asking."

I will say. "Oh thank you for having a good attitude."

- Some will say you're doing a good job, keep doing what you're doing.

- I asked one man downtown. He said, "I Am." I walked across the street, he ran behind me and said thank you for asking. I was having a rough day but when you asked me that I felt better. I thanked the Spirit for letting him feel His presence through me. Asking him if he ever thought about being saved.

- I asked another man and he said yes, he is. Then he said, "Can I buy you a smoothie, it's hot out here." He and his family were tourists, so I accepted and he bought me a smoothie.

- I was witnessing to four young men on the corner. They were smoking marijuana. As I talked to them about the Lord they kept smoking and I was praying silently, Lord please don't let me get high.

- Another time I was witnessing to some guys. They were on one corner selling drugs. I'd be on the other corner witnessing.

- I asked three young ladies as they were going in Kroger. One said she was saved so I witnessed to the other two, then they went in the store. About two minutes later the one that was saved came out and said thank you for witnessing to my friends. When I prayed for her friend at home, I prayed that God will give her boldness to witness.

- I met two Evangelists outside Kroger. I didn't know they were Evangelists. I asked one if she ever thought about being saved and she said all the time. They gave me their numbers, and said they wanted to go witnessing with me next summer. I hope so because I don't see any Christians out witnessing. I met a lady about three years ago. She gives out tracts. I tried to get her to come downtown with me but she didn't.

- Yes, I am saved. You've put a smile on my face.

- One lady said yes. I'm saved, stay cool.

- A couple from out of town took my picture. Some of them would hug me.

- One prophet said you're doing a good thing. Keep it up, I'm praying for you.

- I asked a lady, she said she was saved and she wants to witness to people, so by me asking her she had an idea how to do it.

So saints, we are the true witnesses of Jesus. If you witness to one person a day, a week, or month it's better than not saying anything. Who knows that one you witness to might be saved. God did not save us to keep it to ourselves.

Acts 1:8:
But you will receive power when the Holy Spirit comes on you; and you will be my witnesses in Jerusalem, and in all Judea and Samaria, and to the ends of the earth.

Matthew 28:20:

...And surely I am with you always, to the very end of the age.

BE BLESSED AND GO OUT IN THE NAME OF OUR LORD AND SAVIOUR JESUS CHRIST.

CHAPTER 11

Signs of the End of Time

1 WARS–*Matthew 24:6:*
You will hear of wars and rumors of wars...

There are so many wars going on in other countries that we don't hear about.

2 FAMINES–*Matthew 24:7:*
...There will be famines...

There has always been famines but not in the magnitude we're hearing about all over the world.

3 EARTHQUAKES–*Matthew 24:7:*
...and earthquakes in various places...

Several months ago we had an earthquake that was felt in three states, even Georgia where we don't have earthquakes. There have been earthquakes in states that never had earthquakes before, because the states are not on a fault line. Fault line or not the earthquakes are coming.

4 NATION AGAINST NATION–*Matthew 24:7:*

Nation will rise against nation...

Watch the news. Just about everyday there is conflict with nations.

5 WICKEDNESS WILL INCREASE–*Matthew 24:12:*

Because of the increase of wickedness, the love of most will grow cold.

Mark 13:12:
Brother will betray brother to death, and a father his child. Children will rebel against their parents and have them put to death.

6 FALSE PROPHETS–*Matthew 24:11:*

and many false prophets will appear and deceive many people.

7 MANY WILL TURN AWAY–*1 Timothy 4:1*

The Spirit clearly says that in later times some will abandon the faith and follow deceiving spirits and things taught by demons.

2 Timothy 3:1-5:
But mark this: There will be terrible times in the last days. People will be lovers of themselves, lovers of money, boastful, proud, abusive, disobedient to their parents, ungrateful, unholy, without love, unforgiving, slanderous, without self-control, brutal, not lovers of the good, treacherous, rash, conceited, lovers of pleasure rather than lovers of God—having a form of godliness but denying its power...

8 SIGNS IN THE SKY–*Luke 21:25-28:*

"There will be signs in the sun, moon and stars. On the earth, nations will be in anguish and perplexity at the roaring and tossing of the sea. People will faint from terror, apprehensive of what is coming on the world, for the heavenly bodies will be shaken. At that time they will see

the Son of Man coming in a cloud with power and great glory. When these things begin to take place, stand up and lift up your heads, because your redemption is drawing near."

1 Thessalonians 4:14-18:

For we believe that Jesus died and rose again, and so we believe that God will bring with Jesus those who have fallen asleep in him. According to the Lord's word, we tell you that we who are still alive, who are left until the coming of the Lord, will certainly not precede those who have fallen asleep. For the Lord himself will come down from heaven, with a loud command, with the voice of the archangel and with the trumpet call of God, and the dead in Christ will rise first. After that, we who are still alive and are left will be caught up together with them in the clouds to meet the Lord in the air. And so we will be with the Lord forever. Therefore encourage one another with these words.

2 Thessalonians 1:7-10:

And to you who are troubled rest with us, when the Lord Jesus shall be revealed from heaven with his mighty angels, In flaming fire taking vengeance on them that know not God, and that obey not the gospel of our Lord Jesus Christ: Who shall be punished with everlasting destruction from the presence of the Lord, and from the glory of his power; When he shall come to be glorified in his saints, and to be admired in all them that believe...KJV

Matthew 24:36-39 & 44:

But of that day and hour knoweth no man, no, not the angels of heaven, but my Father only. But as the days of Noah were, so shall also the coming of the Son of man be. For as in the days that were before the flood they were eating and drinking, marrying and giving in marriage, until the day that Noe entered into the ark, And knew not until the flood came, and took them all away; so shall also the coming of the Son of man be.

Therefore be ye also ready: for in such an hour as ye think not the Son of man cometh. KJV

**Watch and pray. Jesus is coming back!
WILL YOU BE READY?**

262 THAT'S NOT IN MY FORECAST:

"Have you ever thought about being saved?" I asked.

"I am," the young lady answered.

"Do you have the Holy Spirit?" I asked.

"Yes," she replied.

Then I asked the man. He said, "That's not in my forecast." And he walked off.

ABOUT THE AUTHOR

Brenda Williams is married with three children. She lives in Savannah Georgia. She was ordained an Evangelist in 2002 but has been going out witnessing since 1998 in stores, on corners, and downtown Savannah. This is the job God has given me to do and I love it!

www.saintsneedtowitness.com

~~101~~ NO 262 REASONS WHY THE
SAINTS NEED TO WITNESS!

www.ingramcontent.com/pod-product-compliance
Lightning Source LLC
Chambersburg PA
CBHW070753100426
42742CB00012B/2120